DICTION

EFFECTIVE SENTENCES

# A Brief
# Handbook
# of English

# A Brief Handbook of English

## Hulon Willis

*Bakersfield College*

HARCOURT BRACE JOVANOVICH, INC.

New York / Chicago / San Francisco / Atlanta

*For Sara*

© 1975 by Harcourt Brace Jovanovich, Inc.

ISBN: 0-15-505559-3

Library of Congress Catalog Card Number: 74-33003

Printed in the United States of America

# Contents

# CONTENTS

CONTENTS

CONTENTS

# Preface

*A Brief Handbook of English* is also available in a variant version that includes a section on the research paper.

This text is a concise reference guide to usage and grammar for beginning writers. It is designed to help them improve the conciseness, clarity, and correctness of their writing. With the book's usefulness foremost in my mind, I have concentrated on the writing problems most troublesome to students. I have avoided subtleties such as "squinting modifiers" and disputed areas of usage such as "reason is because," and have given short explanations—rather than exhaustive analyses—of why the rules are what they are. As much as possible I have avoided discussing options in various aspects of usage, in order not to confuse students or bog them down in a consideration of exceptions. For example, I simply state the rule that a comma is used to separate independent clauses joined by a coordinating conjunction. If a student inserts such a comma in one of the rare cases when it is not needed, no error will be marked; but if the book were to give a full explanation of options, the student might become confused. For this reason I have given concise rules and instructions without splitting hairs. One of my basic assumptions in preparing this book is that in one semester an average student cannot master the basics *and also* many of the refinements of writing. I have restricted myself to the basics. The book, I hope, is not overly prescriptive, but it does take a positive stance in presenting basic rules that the student can rely on.

In so far as is possible, each section of the book is self-contained and offers a minimum of technical explanations. Still, many common grammatical terms must be used in such a reference guide. Students using the book in a non-sequential way may encounter unfamiliar terms that are not explained at that point. Since it is impractical to define terms fully each time they are used, I have included a long opening chapter that explains the basic system of English grammar as scholarly-traditional grammarians see it. I have, however, omitted aspects of grammar that do not have a bearing on the teaching of usage and composition. The book can be used with profit even if Chapter 1 is ignored altogether, but many instructors will want their students to become familiar with the organization and content of this chapter at the beginning of the composition course. The chapter is designed to be a reference book within a reference book. Students can use it easily, since the book's outside back cover indexes all the grammatical terms defined in Chapter 1. The Instructor's Manual contains some exercises on Chapter 1, so that a teacher who wishes may use Chapter 1 and the whole book as a teaching text as well as a reference text.

The Instructor's Manual also contains tests. Since virtually every school nowadays has means of quick reproduction of exercises and tests, it seemed practical to make these available in this form. Instructors may ignore the Manual or may use its materials as their own. The preface to the Manual explains its nature in detail.

Two different correction charts are provided for the teacher's use in guiding the student's revisions. One chart gives number-letter symbols according to the book's organization, with the name of the error or weakness accompanying the number-letter symbol. Teachers who use this chart will therefore make such marks as 3A, 10C, 22D, and so forth on the student's paper, and the student will know which section to refer to for guidance. This chart can also be used more generally, as when the instructor uses the number 10 to indicate an error in the use of the comma without specifying which rule has been violated.

The other chart is composed of traditional symbols, such as *agr, DM, W,* and so on, with the full name of the error following the symbol. The section of the handbook devoted to that error is identified in parentheses after the name of the error. Thus instructors who do not want to use number-letter symbols have a traditional correction chart available to them. The student will find both systems equally usable.

Except where such use would serve no purpose, I have used student writing for examples, on the theory that such examples will ring true to the student when an artificial example might not. In giving a revised version of a student sentence containing an error, I have corrected the error only and have not tried to improve the sentence in other ways. To change more than the error under discussion would, I think, distract the student. Still, the revisions are not *bad* sentences that might adversely affect the student's future writing. Every example is clearly labeled *wrong, right, poor style,* and so on, to eliminate any possibility of confusion.

Two sections of the book may be called glossaries. Section 16G is composed of homophones—such as *course* and *coarse*—and other words that are often confused in spelling but not in meaning. Section 22B is composed of words often confused in meaning—such as *infer* and *imply.* Both correction charts allow the teacher to refer the student to the glossaries.

HULON WILLIS

# Introduction
# to the Student

This text is a guide to usage and grammar to help you improve the conciseness, clarity, and correctness of your writing. Primarily, you will use it as a reference book. It is designed so that your teacher can refer you to particular sections that will explain an error or weakness in your writing and give you guidance in revision. You may also be given exercises and exams to test your mastery of various sections of the book. Even when you are not using the book to revise one of your papers, you may use it to look up rules of punctuation, capitalization, spelling, and so on, so that your paper will require less revision.

Explanations of various rules and instructions about writing require the use of some grammatical terms. You may not be familiar with all of them. Therefore the first chapter is a simplified explanation of the basic system of

English grammar. You will probably not be required to read this chapter all at once, but you should skim it to see what information it contains and how that information is organized. Read the sections that you think you need, and return to the chapter as necessary throughout your course. So that you may use this chapter for quick reference, the outside back cover of the book lists alphabetically, with page numbers, all the grammatical terms defined in Chapter 1. Thus if you need to find out what, say, a conjunctive adverb is, you can refer to the index on the back cover and then to the page in Chapter 1 that clearly explains what a conjunctive adverb is. This chapter avoids grammatical terms and concepts that are not useful in the teaching of usage and composition.

# SECTION ONE

# GRAMMAR

# 1

# Introduction:
# The Basic System
# of English Grammar

Since this text is a reference book, you will not be studying
or referring to its chapters in sequence. Instead, on any particular day you may refer first to, say, Chapter 24, then
Chapter 3, then Chapter 12, and so on. Thus you need to
know some basic grammatical terms before you begin to
use this book. This introductory chapter contains simple
definitions, with brief examples, of the basic terms you need
to know in order to use this book with ease and profit. Probably you already know some of these terms, and maybe all
of them, but here they are for your reference, review, or
study, should your teacher suggest that. Think of this chapter as a reference book within a reference book. Become
familiar with it now, and refer to it for help whenever problems arise in your writing. All of the important terms in it are
listed alphabetically with page references on the outside
back cover.

# 1A   PARTS OF SPEECH

Our language is composed of words, and each word is a part of speech. We recognize words as particular parts of speech by their form or their function, or both. Parts of speech have characteristic forms and functions: nouns serve as subjects and complements, adjectives modify nouns and pronouns, and so on. Yet in actual sentences, nouns and even verbs sometimes modify nouns. Thus parts of speech must be classified **by function** as well as by form. Examples:

ADJECTIVE MODIFYING NOUN: a **pretty** dress
NOUN MODIFYING NOUN: a **cotton** dress
VERB MODIFYING NOUN: a **soaking** dress
DETERMINER MODIFYING NOUN: **her** dress

Knowing that parts of speech may be classified by form and by function will help you use some chapters in this book more profitably. Further illustration of this dual classification, with names of the parts of speech by function, will be given in Section 1E.

The four parts of speech by form that carry the vast bulk of meaning in our language—**nouns, verbs, adjectives,** and **adverbs**—are known as **content words.** They will be defined next. Since these parts of speech are difficult to define, we will briefly discuss several characteristics of each. After a little practice you will come to have a natural feeling for which words are nouns, verbs, adjectives, and adverbs, if you do not already.

## 1A1   Nouns

One quite satisfactory definition of *noun* is that it is the name of anything that exists or that can be conceived. Thus such "names" as *chaos, time, love,* and *apple* are nouns.

Almost every noun can either be made plural or possessive or both. Examples:

one **game**        two **games**
one **ox**          two **oxen**
**golf**'s contribution to the sports world
**concentration**'s effect on the mind
the **Harrises**' wedding anniversary

In these ways nouns can be identified by form.

Almost all nouns can be meaningfully preceded by one of the indefinite articles, *a* or *an;* or by the definite article, *the;* or by a possessive word such as *my, your,* or *John's.* Examples:

a **drink**        the **whisky**        Fred's **pride**
my **love**        her **hose**         Julia's **devotion**

Do not let intervening words—as in *a crisp, sweet apple*—keep you from understanding how *a, an, the, my,* and so on announce the presence of a noun.

Finally, certain word endings, or suffixes, added to other parts of speech form nouns. (Such suffixes are occasionally added to nouns also.) A knowledge of these suffixes will help you get a natural feeling for nouns. Here are the most common, with the suffixes in boldface:

mile + **age** = mileage
deny + **al** = denial
appear + **ance** = appearance
assist + **ant** = assistant
beg + **ar** = beggar
dull + **ard** = dullard
purify + **cation** = purification
secret + **cy** = secrecy
king + **dom** = kingdom
refer + **ee** = referee
superintend + **ent** = superintendent
advise + **er** = adviser
China + **ese** = Chinese

boy + **hood** = boyhood
just + **ice** = justice
act + **ion** = action
social + **ism** = socialism
commune + **ist** = communist
labor + **ite** = laborite
active + **ity** = activity
achieve + **ment** = achievement
lovely + **ness** = loveliness
counsel + **or** = counselor
slave + **ry** = slavery
kin + **ship** = kinship
dissent + **sion** = dissension
introduce + **tion** = introduction
fail + **ure** = failure

These word endings are known as **noun-forming suffixes.**
   Knowledge of all the above characteristics of nouns will
help you in identifying this part of speech.

## 1A2   Verbs

Verbs are words that express an action or a state of being.
Usually, a verb gives an indication of the time of occurrence
of the action or state of being. This indication is called
tense. For example, the noun —

   a fight

expresses an action but no time of occurrence. But in —

   José **will fight** fairly

or

   Sara **fights** viciously,

the same word used as a verb specifies a time of occurrence. (Note that a verb may be one word or more than one
word. In the first sentence, "will fight" is the verb.)
   Verbs, however, are most easily identified by form. With
a very few exceptions, every verb in English has an *ing* form

and a singular, present-tense form ending in *s* or *es*. Also every verb has either a regular *(ed)* or irregular past-tense and past-participle form. Thus virtually every English verb will fit this framework (called a paradigm):

| infinitive | third-person singular, present tense | present participle | past tense | past participle |
|---|---|---|---|---|
| to hug | hugs | hugging | hugged | hugged |
| to break | breaks | breaking | broke | broken |

For simplicity, we can say that any word that takes the *ing* suffix and the *s* suffix to make the singular present tense is a verb.

For proper use of this text you need to know the three categories of verbs and three of their special functions. The three categories of verbs are as follows:

**a. Intransitive verbs** An intransitive verb is an action verb that, in a sentence, does not have a direct object. The subject performs an action without anybody or anything receiving the action. Examples:

INTRANSITIVE VERBS: Quincy **smokes** frequently.
This can opener never **works.**
Melissa **smiled** at me.

Modifiers, such as the adverbs *frequently* and *never* and the prepositional phrase *at me,* do not prevent a verb from being intransitive. The pronoun *me* is the object of the preposition, not a direct object of the verb.

**b. Transitive verbs** A transitive verb is an action verb that, in a sentence, takes a direct object; that is, the action is performed on someone or something. Examples:

TRANSITIVE VERBS: Lucy **smokes** cigars.
Maury **beats** his wife.

*Cigars* and *his wife* are direct objects. Some verbs are intransitive in some sentences and transitive in others.

**c. Linking verbs** Linking verbs are state-of-being verbs, such as *to be, to seem, to appear, to become, to look,* *to taste, to sound, to remain.* Linking verbs are followed either by a predicate noun, which tells what the subject is or seems to be, or by a predicate adjective, which describes the subject. Examples:

LINKING VERBS: Julius **is** a weirdo.
Mr. Merle **became** dogcatcher.
Shirley **looks** pregnant.
Barry **remained** calm.

*Weirdo* and *dogcatcher* are predicate nouns, and *pregnant* and *calm* are predicate adjectives.

Some verbs can function as either intransitive, transitive, or linking. Examples:

INTRANSITIVE: The tree **grew** slowly. (no direct object)
TRANSITIVE: George **grew** a beard. (direct object *beard*)
LINKING: My date **grew** restless. (predicate adjective *restless*)

Linking verbs cause some special writing problems, which are covered in later chapters.

The three special functions of verbs that you need to know are the following:

**d. Tense**   Tense is the function of verbs that specifies time of occurrence. The tense system in English is immensely complex, but for use of this book you need to know only whether a verb form contains one of the past, present, or future tenses. Examples:

PAST TENSES: My horse **vanished** last night.
The cops **had left** before I **returned.**

PRESENT TENSES: I **am telling** you the truth.
Shelley usually **studies** after midnight.

FUTURE TENSES: Times **will get** better.
Maurice **is going to plead** guilty.

**e. Voice**   Voice has to do with whether a subject performs or receives an action. Only action verbs have voice. If in a sentence the subject performs the action, the verb and sentence are said to be in the **active voice.** Example:

ACTIVE VOICE: Benny **mugged** an old man for six pennies.

If the subject receives the action, the verb and sentence are said to be in the **passive voice.** Example:

PASSIVE VOICE: An old man **was mugged** for six pennies.

If the doer of the action in a passive-voice sentence is mentioned, he is named in a *by* phrase; e.g., *by Benny* could be attached to the preceding example sentence. A passive-voice verb always has a form of *to be* in it.

**f. Mood** Mood is the function of a verb that expresses the speaker's attitude toward the factuality or likelihood of what he says. The **indicative mood** expresses a fact or what is believed to be a fact. Example:

INDICATIVE MOOD: Ricky **makes** more money stealing than I **do** working.

The **subjunctive mood** indicates condition contrary to fact, or doubt, potentiality, desirability, obligation, and other such nonfactual concepts. Examples:

SUBJUNCTIVE MOOD: I wish I **were** a member of the Realities.
I suggested that he **keep** quiet. (Note that *keeps* won't function here properly even though *he* is singular.)
You **should marry** a second wife.

The **imperative mood** states a request or command. Examples:

IMPERATIVE MOOD: **Get** off my back.
**Scatter** before we're caught.

There are other functions of verbs, but the foregoing are the ones that have to do with writing problems discussed in later chapters.

## 1A3 Adjectives

An adjective is a describing word; it describes (or modifies) a noun or pronoun. But other parts of speech—such as the noun *comedian* and the verb *stumbles*—also carry an element of description. Thus *adjective* is very hard to define. But an understanding of the following characteristics of adjectives will give you a feel for identifying them.

First, almost all adjectives can be **compared** with *er* (or *more*) and *est* (or *most*). Examples:

| *stem* | *comparative form* | *superlative form* |
|--------|--------------------|--------------------|
| sweet | sweeter | sweetest |
| beautiful | more beautiful | most beautiful |

But since adverbs also can be compared, more is needed to identify adjectives by form. Thus if a word can be compared *and* (1) can have *ly* added to make an adverb *or* (2) can have *ness* added to make a noun, it is an adjective. Examples:

| clear | clearer | clearest | clearly |
|-------|---------|----------|---------|
| mean | meaner | meanest | meanness |

Words fitting these two requirements are always adjectives. In comparing some adjectives (or adverbs) *more* and *most* are used instead of *er* and *est* solely to make the word sound smooth rather than awkward. *Beautifulest* is awkward, while *most beautiful* is smooth. The comparative *(er)* and superlative *(est)* forms of *good* and *well* are the irregular *better* and *best;* of *bad* and *ill* they are the irregular *worse* and *worst*.

Another easy test to help you get the feel of the adjective is to see that adjectives fit this pattern (any common noun can be used instead of *student*):

That _____ student is very _____.

Examples:

That **bright** student is very **bright**.
That **obscene** joke is very **obscene**.

Almost always when a word fits this pattern it is an adjective by form, and almost all adjectives will fit the pattern.

Here is another easy test to identify adjectives:

He (she, it) seems _____.

Virtually every word *except a noun* that will fit this slot is an adjective. Examples:

> He seems **up-tight.**
> She seems **virtuous.**
> It seems **dead.**

An understanding of this structural position of the adjective will improve your ability to recognize that part of speech automatically.

Finally, we use a number of suffixes to convert other parts of speech (and occasionally other adjectives) into adjectives. Here are the most common, with the suffixes in boldface:

> read + **able** = readable
> person + **al** = personal
> Africa + **an** = African
> resist + **ant** = resistant
> fortune + **ate** = fortunate
> conserve + **ative** = conservative
> exist + **ent** = existent
> sin + **ful** = sinful
> athlete + **ic** = athletic
> boy + **ish** = boyish
> assert + **ive** = assertive
> mercy + **less** = merciless
> bird + **like** = birdlike
> lone + **ly** = lonely
> prohibit + **ory** = prohibitory
> courage + **ous** = courageous
> quarrel + **some** = quarrelsome
> shine + **y** = shiny

These word endings are known as **adjective-forming suffixes.** Understanding them will help you develop a feel for identifying adjectives. Be sure to note that the suffix *ly* forms only a few adjectives; in most cases that suffix changes an adjective into an adverb. If a word ending in *ing* or *ed*—such as *interesting* and *excited*—can be modified by *very,* it is an adjective.

## 1A4 Adverbs

Like the adjective, the adverb is a describing word. Its most common function is to describe (or modify) a verb, telling how, when, or where. (Also, adverbs sometimes modify adjectives and other adverbs.) The so-called "pure" adverbs are those that are formed from adjectives by the addition of the suffix *ly*. Examples:

| *adjective* | *adverb* |
|---|---|
| rapid | rapidly |
| sweet | sweetly |
| loving | lovingly |
| excited | excitedly |

Like adjectives, such adverbs can be ccmpared. Examples:

| *stem* | *comparative form* | *superlative form* |
|---|---|---|
| bitterly | more bitterly | most bitterly |
| happily | more happily | most happily |

This is the easy way to recognize most English adverbs, but you should be careful not to confuse the few *ly* adjectives — *kindly, lovely, friendly, timely,* and a few others — with adverbs.

The difference between adjectives and adverbs is illustrated in these two sentences:

ADJECTIVE: John looked **curious.**
ADVERB: John looked **curiously.**

The first sentence (with *looked* as a linking verb) describes the appearance of John. The second (with *looked* as an intransitive verb) tells the manner in which John looked at something.

English also has a number of so-called "flat" adverbs that do not end in *ly* but that do usually modify verbs. Most of them express either time or place. The most common ones are *soon, never, often, there, here, upward, well* (which is also an adjective), *inside, now, seldom, always, somewhere, behind, above,* and some other words like these.

A useful fact to know about adverbs is that most of them express **time, place,** or **manner** and thus can have the words *then, there,* and *thus* substituted for them. Examples:

I'll come **sometime.** = I'll come **then.**
I can't find the jam **anywhere.** = I can't find the jam **there.**
She smiled **wickedly.** = She smiled **thus.**

However, words and word groups that are not adverbs by form also modify verbs, and they may meaningfully have *then, there,* or *thus* substituted for them. Examples:

Cheryl came **home.** = there   (*Home* is a noun.)
We'll call **at ten o'clock.** = then   (*At ten o'clock* is a prepositional phrase.)
Hemingway wrote **standing.** = thus   (*Standing* is a verb.)

In Section 1E we will make modification clearer, but understanding the above characteristics of adverbs will give you a feel for identifying them. Some important writing problems are concerned with the distinction between adjectives and adverbs.

## 1A5   Structure Words

The vast majority of words in English are nouns, verbs, adjectives, and adverbs. As content words, they are **open classes,** which means that new words (or new definitions of old words) enter these classes frequently, thus expanding the English vocabulary. A much smaller number of words, but a larger number of parts of speech, are called **structure words.** Even though most of these words carry some meaning, their chief function is to provide a framework for arranging the many nouns, verbs, adjectives, and adverbs into meaningful sentences. The structure words all belong to **closed classes,** because new ones very rarely enter the language. There are many kinds of structure words, and there is much overlapping in the groups. (That is, one word, such as *that,* may belong to several groups.) Their grammatical behavior is complex. We will mention and briefly define only those of which you need an elementary knowledge in order to use this text as a reference handbook. What follows is only a very small part of the total grammar of structure words, the part that will be useful to you.

**a. Determiners**  Words that signal that a noun is coming are called determiners. They determine something about the nature of the noun that follows. Sometimes two determiners precede a noun. A few single determiners consist of two words. Here are examples of the chief determiners:

| | | |
|---|---|---|
| **a** bottle | **John's** hangover | **all** prisons |
| **an** oyster | **this** remedy | **every** chance |
| **the** grape | **no** money | **such a** pity |
| **my** beer | **some** disease | **all the** excuses |

The words in boldface may be thought of as noun markers. Any **noun marker** like these is a determiner. Of course other words may come between the determiner and its noun, as in *a silly old man.*

Incidentally, the list above shows how parts of speech may be labeled differently as their functions differ. While *John's* is a determiner here, *John* is commonly a noun; *all* and *some* can be pronouns, and so on.

**b. Prepositions**  A preposition is a kind of connective that shows a relationship between two words. The second word is usually a noun or noun substitute which functions as the object of the preposition and helps form a prepositional phrase. (Prepositional phrases are discussed in more detail in Section 1B1.) Examples, with the prepositions in boldface and the prepositional phrases underlined:

| | |
|---|---|
| the man **with** the hoe | different **from** mine |
| the time **of** day | do it **for** me |
| a trip **to** the islands | conducted **by** the composer |

You would be very hard pressed to give a clear definition of *with, from, of,* and *for* in these constructions; they are structure, not content, words. However, most prepositions do have some meaning. In using a number of the chapters of this text you will need to recognize prepositional phrases. Here are the most common single-word prepositions:

| | | | |
|---|---|---|---|
| above | besides | into | through |
| across | between | like | till |
| after | beyond | near | to |
| along | but | of | toward(s) |
| among | by | off | under |
| around | down | on | until |
| at | during | outside | upon |
| before | for | over | with |
| behind | from | past | within |
| below | in | save | without |
| beside | inside | since | |

We also have compound prepositions in English, of which the following are the most common:

| | | |
|---|---|---|
| ahead of | contrary to | instead of |
| apart from | due to | on account of |
| as for | for the sake of | out of |
| as well as | in addition to | owing to |
| aside from | in back of | rather than |
| away from | in case of | together with |
| because of | in front of | up at |
| belonging to | in place of | up on |
| by means of | in spite of | up to |
| by way of | inside of | with regard to |

Some of these compound prepositions—as in the construction *in addition to the money*—can be analyzed as forming two prepositional phrases rather than one phrase with a compound preposition.

**c. Verb auxiliaries**  Many verbs are composed of two or more words, the last word being the main verb and the others being auxiliaries that specify tense and other meanings. Examples, with the auxiliaries in boldface:

**have been** going  **will be** gone
**could have** gone  **should have been** going

15

The number of possible combinations of auxiliaries in English verb forms is enormous. Fortunately, in order to use this text, you need only recognize auxiliaries, not understand their complex grammar.

The verbs *to be, to do,* and *to have* have meanings in English and can function as sentence verbs. But forms of these verbs also function as auxiliaries, with their meanings being entirely different from their meanings as regular verbs. For example, in —

I **have** some beans,

*have* has the meaning of *possess.* But in —

I **have** roasted some beans,

*have* has no such meaning. It is an auxiliary verb that helps to convey tense. The case is similar with *to be* and *to do.* These forms of *to be, to do,* and *to have* function as verb auxiliaries:

> *to be:* be, am, is, are, was, were, being, *and* been
> *to do:* do, does, *and* did
> *to have:* has, have, having, *and* had

Examples:

> Joseph **has been** studying for an hour.
> Molly **does** respect her parents.

Another group of words are called **modal auxiliaries.** Although they are used with a main verb, they carry meaning of their own. The chief modal auxiliaries are the following:

| can | may | must | shall | will |
|-----|-----|------|-------|------|
| could | might | ought to | should | would |

Examples:

> I **may** leave early, but you **ought to** help the committee.

The modals carry some tense meaning and also express subtle meanings of intent, possibility, obligation, condition, and so on.

**d. Coordinating connectives** A coordinating connective joins two grammatical constructions equal in rank, such as two nouns, two prepositional phrases, or two independent clauses. Many of the chapters in this text will refer to them. Two classes of these connectives are to be identified:

**Coordinating conjunctions** (with two exceptions) may be used to join pairs of many kinds of constructions, from single words to independent clauses. (Clauses will be discussed more fully later in this chapter.) They are the following:

| | | |
|---|---|---|
| and | or | both . . . and |
| but | nor | not only . . . but (also) |
| yet | for | either . . . or |
| | so | neither . . . nor |

*For* and *so* can be used to join only independent clauses. The two-part conjunctions are also called **correlatives.**

**Conjunctive adverbs** are coordinating connectives that join only independent clauses. They are the following:

| | | |
|---|---|---|
| accordingly | furthermore | otherwise |
| afterward(s) | hence | still |
| also | however | then |
| besides | later | therefore |
| consequently | moreover | thus |
| earlier | nevertheless | |

Both kinds of coordinating connectives express such relationships as **contrast, cause-and-result, accumulation, condition,** and **time.** When a coordinating connective joins two independent clauses, each could stand by itself as a full, complete sentence, for a sentence may begin with a coordinating connective.

**e. Subordinating conjunctions** A subordinating conjunction is a connective that expresses a relationship between two ideas that are not equal in rank. That is, one of the ideas can stand by itself as a sentence, but the idea introduced by the subordinating conjunction cannot. If let stand by itself, it would be a nonsentence, or a sentence fragment. Many words that are subordinating conjunctions in some sentence can be prepositions or other connectives in other sentences. You will recall that there is much overlapping of structure words in English. For reference, here is a list of subordinating conjunctions:

| | | |
|---|---|---|
| after | if | since |
| although | in case (that) | so long as |
| as | in order that | so (that) |
| as . . . as | in that | than |
| as if | inasmuch as | though |
| as long as | less than | unless |
| as soon as | like | until |
| as though | more than | when |
| because | no matter how | where |
| before | now that | whereas |
| even though | once | while |
| fewer than | provided (that) | |

The subordinating conjunctions are very important words that express such relationships as **cause-and-result, contrast, condition, manner** or **method, purpose, time,** and **place.** To use this reference handbook fully, you need a basic understanding of them.

**f. Pronouns**    A pronoun is defined as a word that stands for a noun, the noun being the pronoun's **antecedent.** But the English pronoun system is far more complex than that definition indicates. The pronoun system causes so many writing problems that it will be dealt with in several chapters of this book. Here, we will identify five kinds of pronouns: personal, relative, interrogative, demonstrative, and indefinite.

The **personal pronouns** have **case,** which means that they change their forms according to their use in sentences. There are three cases in English: (1) the **subjective,** (2) the **objective,** and (3) the **possessive.** Here are the case forms of the personal pronouns:

| *subjective case* | *objective case* | *possessive case* |
|---|---|---|
| I | me | my, mine |
| you | you | your, yours |
| he | him | his |
| she | her | her, hers |
| it | it | its |
| we | us | our, ours |
| they | them | their, theirs |

The personal pronouns also have **reflexive** forms, as follows:

| | |
|---|---|
| myself | himself |
| ourselves | herself |
| yourself | itself |
| yourselves | themselves |

The chief **relative pronouns** are *who* (subjective case), *whom* (objective case), *whose* (possessive case), *which,* and *that.* (These last two do not have case.) A relative pronoun is used to connect (or relate) a dependent clause to another part of a sentence. Example:

There's the cop **who** busted me.

The antecedent of *who* is *cop. Who* introduces the clause and relates it to the first part of the sentence. The relative pronouns, then, are connectives. In a complex grammatical way they join ideas to each other.

Sometimes a relative pronoun is not stated but is understood in a sentence. Example:

The course I like best is Marriage and Family Life.

The relative pronoun *that,* with *course* as its antecedent, is understood before *I.*

*Who* and *whom* are also **interrogative** (question-forming) pronouns. They pose a writing problem that is discussed in Section 5C.

The **demonstrative pronouns** are the "pointing" pronouns *this, that, these,* and *those.* They may be used with nouns (as determiners) or by themselves, with the nouns understood. Examples:

> **This** pornography seems mild today.
> **That** is the one I want.

In the second sentence, whatever subject is under discussion is understood after *that*.

*This* and *that* are also used in a more general way to refer to whole ideas. Examples:

RIGHT: I expected Professor Sneed to flunk me, and **that** is what he did.

RIGHT: We are out of cash again. **This** is getting to be a common occurrence.

In these examples, both *that* and *this* have whole ideas as their antecedents.

There is also a sizable group of words in English known as **indefinite pronouns.** They function as nouns but make indefinite reference to people or things.

| | | |
|---|---|---|
| one | anybody | another |
| no one | everybody | one another |
| anyone | nobody | each other |
| everyone | somebody | anyone else (and |
| someone | other | others with *else*) |

**g. Qualifiers**   A small group of words that modify adjectives and adverbs are called qualifiers because they qualify, or limit in some way, the meaning of adjectives and adverbs. Some colloquial qualifiers, discussed in Section 20B, should be avoided in semiformal writing. (Most college writing may be classed as semiformal.) The chief qualifiers used in semiformal writing are the following:

| | | | |
|---|---|---|---|
| very | somewhat | fairly | a little |
| rather | especially | wholly | quite |

# 1B  SENTENCES

The parts of speech defined in Section 1A are variously arranged, of course, to form sentences. Every sentence is composed of a **subject** and **predicate,** and every predicate contains a verb. A predicate may or may not contain a **complement,** which is a word or word group that completes a meaning begun in the verb.

## 1B1  Subjects

The **subject** of a sentence is the person, thing, or concept that performs the action stated in the verb if the verb is in the active voice or that receives the action if the verb is in the passive voice (see Section 1A2e) or that is in the state of being expressed by a linking verb (see Section 1A2c). A simple test for determining the subject of a sentence is to ask who or what about the verb. Examples:

Our team won the championship.

Who won? *Our team*, which is therefore the subject.

The championship was won by our team.

What was won? *The championship*, which is the subject.

Sally appears dazed.

Who appears? *Sally*, which is the subject.

Sometimes the subject is a noun with many modifiers. Such a noun and all of its modifiers together form the **complete subject.** Example:

Any high official of the United States government can be impeached.

Who can be impeached? *Any high official of the United States government*, which is the complete subject. The central noun (also known as the headword) in such a long subject is known as the **simple subject.** It — and it alone — controls the verb. Example:

> Any member of a nudist camp that is affiliated with other camps can have free access to those camps too.

Who can have free access? *Any member,* which is the simple subject within the complete subject. (The complete subject is all of the words preceding *can have.*)

A good point to remember is that in the vast majority of English sentences the subject precedes the verb. Two rather frequent exceptions are sentences that begin with *there* and *it* as expletives (fillers without meaning). Examples, with the complete subjects in boldface:

> There is **no way to form a compound out of helium and hydrogen.**

What is? The whole boldface construction is, with *no way* as the simple subject.

> It is true **that Doug jilted Maggie.**

What is true? The whole boldface noun clause, which is the subject. (There is no single-word simple subject in such sentences.) Some writers do at times use inverted sentence order; but usually asking who or what about the verb will tell you the subject.

## 1B2   Predicates

The predicate of a sentence is the verb and its complement, if it has one, plus any modifiers (see Section 1E). Examples, with the predicates in boldface:

> The bee **stung Uncle Wilhelm.**
> Pete **can run very fast.**
> The young mother **screamed at the teenagers bullying her children.**

The headword in the predicate is always the verb (which may be one or more words). The verb must be what is called

**finite,** that is, it must be a form that can serve as a sentence verb. Some examples of finite verbs are the following:

Jess **has been going** to a psychiatrist for a year now.
He **is profiting** from his treatment.
His parents **aren't.**

Verb forms that cannot function as sentence verbs are known as **nonfinite.** Some examples are *known, been gone,* and *having escaped.* You can see that the following groups of words are not sentences:

We known about the fire
Shirley been gone now for two days

The addition of verb auxiliaries would make these verbs finite and make correct sentences:

We **should have known** about the fire.
Shirley **has been gone** now for two days.

Many predicates have **complements** of the verbs—that is, words or constructions that complete a meaning initiated in the verb. To use this book effectively, you need to understand only four kinds of complements:

**a. Direct objects**   A direct object is the person or thing that receives the action of a transitive verb. Examples:

DIRECT OBJECTS: Jonesy lit his **cigar.**
The transcriber omitted an **expletive.**

**b. Indirect objects**   An indirect object normally occurs only in conjunction with a direct object. It specifies the person or thing to or for whom the action is performed. Examples:

INDIRECT OBJECTS: Hortense gave **me** a kiss.
The deacon told **the preacher** a lie.

*Kiss* and *lie* are direct objects. Indirect objects can always be converted into prepositional phrases beginning with *to* or *for.* Example:

The deacon told a lie **to the preacher.**

In this sentence the indirect object has been replaced by a prepositional phrase.

**c. Predicate nouns**   A predicate noun follows a linking verb and renames the subject in different terms. Examples:

PREDICATE NOUNS: Elsie remained **chairperson** of the English Department.

Susie is a **sweetheart.**

**d. Predicate adjectives**   A predicate adjective follows a linking verb and describes the subject. Examples:

PREDICATE ADJECTIVES:  The moon is **bright** tonight.

Julio became **bitter** as the interview progressed.

In all the examples given above, the complements plus the verbs and modifiers form the sentence predicates.

## 1B3   Kinds of Sentences

Though there seems to be an infinity of different kinds of English sentences, for simplicity we will identify four types.

**a.** **A simple sentence** is one that contains only one independent clause and no dependent clause. (See Section 1D for a description of clauses.) Even though various kinds of phrases carrying additional ideas may be in such a sentence, it is still called simple. Examples:

Glass is a noncrystalline substance.

Without any hesitation, I strode into the panther's cage.

Regardless of its length, a simple sentence has only one subject and one predicate.

**b.** **A compound sentence** is one composed of two or more independent clauses but no dependent clauses. Examples, with the independent clauses in boldface:

**We broke the speed limit without care,** but **the liquor store had already closed.**

**The sun and moon appear to be about the same size;** however, **they are really vastly different in size.**

A compound sentence has at least two subjects and two predicates.

   **c. A complex sentence** is one with one independent clause and one or more dependent clauses. Examples, with the dependent clauses in boldface:

> **While Ruthie kept guard,** I climbed through the transom.
> I won't vote for Mr. Huston **because he slandered minority groups.**
> **If it rains,** we'll call off our race, **since the roadway would be too slippery for our tires.**

   **d. A compound-complex sentence** contains at least two independent clauses and at least one dependent clause. Examples, with the dependent clauses in boldface:

> **If the weather is fair,** we will go on our hunting trip, and I expect us to find much game.
> **Since I could see his hat on the table,** I knew of the intruder's presence, but I made no move **in case he had a pistol.**

This traditional four-fold classification of sentence types does not tell the whole truth about the great variety of structure in English sentences, but it is a useful starting point.

# 1C PHRASES

A phrase is a group of words that function as a unit but that do not have a subject and predicate. You need to understand three kinds of phrases in order to utilize this book fully.

## 1C1 Prepositional Phrases

A prepositional phrase begins with a preposition and closes with the object of the preposition, usually a noun or pronoun. Examples:

PREPOSITIONAL PHRASES: The girl **in the bikini** standing **by the pool's edge** was invited **as an additional guest.**

Prepositional phrases are used as modifiers, like adjectives and adverbs.

## 1C2   Verbal Phrases

A verbal phrase is a verb form plus various other words that go with it to form a unit. Many different verb forms can be headwords in verb phrases, but to use this book you need not know their names. You need only to recognize that a verb form is the headword of the phrase and that the phrase is a unit. Examples:

VERBAL PHRASES: The man **to see about tickets** is Scalper Joe.
**Realizing we were trapped,** we meekly surrendered.
**Known for her generosity,** Carrie was often imposed upon.
**Jogging every morning** helped me lose ten pounds.

Several kinds of errors in sentence structure and punctuation involve verbal phrases.

## 1C3   Noun Phrases

A noun phrase is composed of a noun headword plus all its modifiers. Examples:

NOUN PHRASES: **A list of students serving as student-body officers** was posted in the library.
**A number of spectators at the construction site** offered much advice to the workers.

The headwords in these phrases are *list* and *number;* they govern the whole phrases. You will need to understand the nature of noun phrases to deal with subject-verb agreement.

# 1D CLAUSES

A **clause** is a construction that has a subject and predicate (see Sections 1B1 and 1B2). Clauses are either independent or dependent.

## 1D1 Independent Clauses

An **independent clause** is in effect a simple sentence. It is a clause that can stand alone, beginning with a capital letter and ending with a period or question mark. The material in Sections 1B1 and 1B2 gives you information that applies to independent clauses as well as to sentences.

## 1D2 Dependent Clauses

**Dependent clauses** are like independent clauses in having a subject and a predicate containing a finite verb. They differ in that they begin with subordinating connectives, which keep them from standing alone as complete sentences. *Grammatically,* a dependent clause depends on the rest of the sentence, but, since it has a subject and predicate, it contains a full unit of meaning. There are three kinds of dependent clauses.

**a.** **Adjective clauses** usually begin with one of these relative pronouns, which serve as subordinating connectives: *who, whom, whose, which,* and *that.* Like adjectives, an adjective clause usually modifies a noun or pronoun. In the examples below, each adjective clause modifies the noun it follows.

ADJECTIVE CLAUSES: The guest **who arrives last** will receive a booby prize.

A man **whose wife is beautiful** is always worried.

We elected Sneedby, **who paid two dollars a vote.**

I voted for Scraggs, **to whom I owed a debt.**

The subjects and predicates of these adjective clauses are as follows:

> who / arrives last
> whose wife / is beautiful
> who / paid two dollars a vote
> I / owed a debt to whom

Occasionally an adjective clause can modify the whole idea of a sentence or word group, in which case it must begin with *which*. In this example, the adjective clause, in bold-face, modifies the whole idea of the independent clause:

> The catcher of our team batted .406 this year, **which set a new local record.**

An understanding of adjective clauses is especially important in knowing how to punctuate correctly.

**b. Adverb clauses** begin with one of the subordinating conjunctions listed on page 18. The subordinating conjunction expresses a relationship between the adverb clause and, usually, some other whole idea. Examples:

ADVERB CLAUSES:  **If you drink,** I will drive.
                 I proposed to you **because you are rich.**
                 You will marry me **because I am handsome.**

The subjects and predicates of these adverb clauses are as follows:

> you / drink
> you / are rich
> I / am handsome

The subordinating conjunctions *if* and *because* make the clauses dependent, or keep them from standing alone as complete sentences.

**c. Noun clauses** begin with *that* (a meaningless subordinating connective), with *what,* with a relative pronoun, or with a subordinating conjunction. (Only a few of the subordinating conjunctions can begin noun clauses.) The distinctive characteristic of noun clauses is that they function as nouns in sentences—usually as subjects or direct objects. The best way to test for a noun clause is to see that either *someone* or *something* can be substituted for it. Examples:

NOUN CLAUSES: I know **that you love me.** (I know something.)
**When you leave** is no concern of mine. (Something is no concern of mine.)
**Whoever buys the beer** chooses the music we play. (Someone chooses the music we play.)

The subjects and predicates of these noun clauses are as follows:

>you / love me
>you / leave
>whoever / buys the beer

The *that, when,* and *whoever* prevent the clauses from standing as complete sentences.

A number of the following chapters, especially those on punctuation, will deal with dependent clauses.

# 1E MODIFIERS

A **modifier** is a word or word group that describes, limits, or adds to another word or word group. For example, if to the phrase *a shirt* we add the modifier *blue* to get *a blue shirt,* we have (1) described the shirt to a degree; (2) limited the shirt, since all non-blue shirts are now excluded; and (3) in a sense, added to the shirt, since we have told something about it that formerly we did not know. This all seems simple, but actually modification is one of the most complex aspects of grammar. You need to know some of the aspects of modification in order to deal with many writing problems treated in the following chapters.

There are three general kinds of modifiers. In discussing them we return to the fact that parts of speech are classified by form and by function. Thus some words may function as adjectives or adverbs even though they are classified as other parts of speech. The three general kinds of modifiers are **adjectivals, adverbials,** and **sentence modifiers.**

## 1E1   Adjectivals

Any word or word group that modifies a noun or pronoun is by function an adjectival. Here are examples of various kinds of adjectivals. The adjectival is in boldface and the noun it modifies is underlined:

> the **tastiest** biscuit   [*Tastiest* is an adjective.]
> This cloth feels **smooth.**   [*Smooth* is an adjective.]
> a **paper** tiger   [*Paper* is a noun functioning as an adjectival.]
> a **running** thief   [*Running* is a verb functioning as an adjectival.]
> the apartment **below**   [*Below* is an adverb functioning as an adjectival.]
> the go-go dancer **on stage in the nightclub**   [*On stage* and *in the nightclub* are prepositional phrases functioning as adjectivals.]
> the girl **not wearing a bikini**   [The verbal phrase functions as an adjectival.]
> **Being exhausted,** Joe took a nap.   [The verbal phrase functions as an adjectival.]
> Dr. Smale, **whose specialty is urology**   [The adjective clause functions as an adjectival.]
> a time **when all chickens are asleep**   [The adverb clause functions as an adjectival.]

Although most of the constructions in boldface are not adjectives, they are all adjectivals by function because they modify nouns.

## 1E2   Adverbials

Any word or word group that modifies a verb, adjective, or another adverb is an adverbial by function. Most adverbials answer the questions *Where? When?* or *How?* Here are examples of various kinds of adverbials. The adverbial in each instance is in boldface and the verb it modifies is underlined:

> to peer **cautiously**  [*Cautiously* is an adverb.]
> arrived **yesterday**  [*Yesterday* is a noun functioning as an adverbial.]
> If you study **long,** you study **wrong.**  [*Long* and *wrong* are adjectives functioning as adverbials.]
> frozen **by the north wind**  [The prepositional phrase functions as an adverbial.]
> to eat **standing**  [*Standing* is a verb functioning as an adverbial.]
> I studied hard **to improve my grades.**  [The verb phrase functions as an adverbial.]
> smoking **where it is forbidden**  [The adverb clause functions as an adverbial.]

All of the constructions in boldface are adverbials because they modify verbs.

## 1E3  Sentence Modifiers

In some sentences a modifier modifies not a single word but a whole idea. Then it is a sentence modifier. Here are examples of sentence modifiers, which are in boldface.

> **Happily,** Tweed did not die.  [*Happily* is an adverb modifying the whole sentence. Note how different in meaning this sentence is from "Tweed did not die happily," in which *happily* is an adverbial modifying *die*.]
> **Under the circumstances,** we should engage in plea bargaining.  [The prepositional phrase modifies the whole idea.]
> **Strictly speaking,** the purchase of a new car is not an investment.  [The verbal phrase modifies the whole idea.]
> We invested in common stock, **which is a good way to go broke fast.**  [The dependent clause modifies the first idea.]

In determining what a word or word group modifies, the best approach is to ask *what goes with what.* In sections 1E1 and 1E2, if you will ask this question about the examples, you will see that the boldface construction goes with what is underlined.

# 1F APPOSITIVES

Basically, an **appositive** is a noun repeater; that is, it renames in different words the noun it is **in apposition to.** It gives more information about that noun. An appositive may be a single word, a phrase, or a clause. Examples of appositives, with the appositive in boldface and the noun it is in apposition to underlined:

> Neutron stars, **heavenly bodies with a diameter of only a few miles,** were discovered in the 1970's. [The appositive is a noun phrase.]
> The British writer **John Wilson** may receive a Nobel Prize. [The appositive is a noun.]
> The belief **that like produces like** is an old superstition. [The appositive is a noun clause.]
> Her first love — **eating wild mushrooms** — was her last act. [The appositive is a verbal phrase.]

Sometimes an appositive is in apposition to a whole idea. Example:

> He conceded the election, a **gesture** his backers disapproved of.

The appositive in boldface is in apposition to the underlined sentence. Occasionally appositives are introduced by such connectives as *that is, namely,* and *or.* Example:

> *Vibrissae,* or **whiskers,** grow on the faces of all species of cats and seals.

*Whiskers* is in apposition to *vibrissae.*

Appositives involve important aspects of punctuation and will be considered further in Section II.

# 1G COORDINATION

**Coordination** means the joining of two or more sentence parts or independent clauses so that they are equal in rank.

This grammatical function, which involves problems in punctuation and sentence structure, usually calls for one of the coordinating connectives discussed in Section 1A5d. Parts are said to be **compounded** when they are coordinated; also, we speak of coordinated parts as being **items in a series.** Example of coordination:

> **Riding horses, drinking whisky,** and **writing novels** were William Faulkner's favorite pastimes.

The three phrases in boldface are equal in rank.

# 1H SUBORDINATION

**Subordination** means that one sentence part is unequal in rank to, or is placed beneath, another part. A subordinated phrase or clause is usually introduced by one of the subordinating conjunctions discussed in Section 1A5e or by a relative pronoun or by *that* or *what*. Also, any kind of sentence modifier is a subordinate construction. Example of subordination, with the subordinated clause in boldface:

> Vodka is intoxicating, **though it is free of fusel oils.**

If the *though,* which produces subordination, is changed to *but,* coordination results:

> Vodka is intoxicating, but it is free of fusel oils.

Now the clauses are equal in rank.

Coordination and subordination are involved in various aspects of sentence structure and punctuation. An understanding of coordination and subordination is important for expressing meaning precisely.

# 1I AMBIGUITY

An important term in grammar is **ambiguity.** This means that a sentence has two possible meanings, often without

a clue to show the reader which meaning is intended.
Examples of ambiguity:

> How would you like to see a model home?
> Bathing beauties can be fun.
> During my college career I had thirty odd teachers.
> I will lose no time in reading your manuscript.

Ambiguities can be entertaining, but usually ambiguity is a
grave weakness in writing.

The foregoing are explanations of the basics of English
grammar that pertain to the writing problems to be discussed in the rest of this reference handbook. You may not
need to make much use of this introductory chapter, but it
is here for you, and it may at times answer pressing questions or give you insights that will improve the quality of
your writing.

# Sentence Fragments

A good writer needs to have **sentence sense** to avoid writing in **sentence fragments,** or nonsentences. Sentence sense is the ability to recognize that a construction is either a complete sentence, capable of standing alone, or a sentence fragment that should not stand alone. Sentences, of course, begin with capital letters and end with marks of end punctuation. The person with sentence sense automatically composes in complete sentences, but one who does not have full sentence sense often makes serious errors in writing. These errors are discussed in this chapter and Chapter 3.

Sentence sense is largely intuitive. Many people easily develop sentence sense without fully understanding just why they have it. Some other people have much difficulty in developing it. Generally, people who study grammar, which is compactly presented in our first chapter, develop sentence sense more easily than do those who are unaware of the nature of grammar.

The whole problem of sentence sense is complex and involves oddities. For example, consider the following construction:

While the professor explained the theory of relativity

Every word (except possibly *while*) in that construction contains its own full meaning without reference to a preceding sentence; yet the construction is not a sentence and should not be entered into writing as though it were a sentence. But many constructions that people with sentence sense automatically recognize as sentences cannot, so far as *meaning* is concerned, stand alone, because they must draw meaning from previous sentences through reference. But *grammatically* they can stand alone.

Sentence sense lets us recognize the following:

1. That pronoun reference to a preceding sentence does not prevent a construction from being a sentence. Example:

SENTENCE: He gave it to them.

By itself, this sentence is far from having complete meaning, but it can stand alone.

2. That reference of a verb auxiliary to a preceding sentence does not prevent a construction from being a sentence. Example:

SENTENCE: He could if I did.

The auxiliaries *could* and *did* must draw their meaning from a preceding sentence. Still, in spite of its lack of meaning, this construction is a sentence.

3. That the reference of *so, thus, then,* and *there* to a preceding sentence does not prevent a construction from being a sentence. Example:

SENTENCE: So was Uncle John.

Both *so* and *was* must get their meaning from the preceding sentence.

4. That a construction may begin with a coordinating connective or transitional phrase and still stand alone as a sentence. Examples:

SENTENCES: But she wouldn't.

For example, alcohol can be fermented from potatoes.

Coordinating connectives and transitional phrases are frequently used to begin sentences.

On the other hand, sentence sense lets us recognize the following:

1. That a clause beginning with a subordinating connective (subordinating conjunctions, relative pronouns, and a few connectives such as *that* and *what*) is **not** a sentence. Examples:

NONSENTENCES: Although Elaine is an excellent student.

Because the hot water heater exploded.

What Glenda had in mind.

The subordinating connectives *although, because,* and *what* keep these meaningful subject-predicate combinations from being sentences.

2. That a construction without a subject and predicate is not a sentence. Examples:

NONSENTENCES: To be free. To live in peace.

Without contributing a nickel.

Mercilessly unfair to all.

Though these constructions deliver more meaning than, say, the sentence *he could,* they are not sentences because they do not have subject-predicate combinations.

If you find that you need to refer to this chapter or Chapter 3 very often, you need to work on developing your sentence sense. You should carefully study Sections 1B and 1D and perhaps all of Chapter 1.

# 2A   DETACHED CLAUSES AS SENTENCE FRAGMENTS

**Write in complete sentences; do not let a dependent clause stand as a sentence.**

A common kind of sentence fragment is a **detached dependent clause** which, instead of standing by itself with a beginning capital letter and end punctuation, should be attached to the preceding sentence, sometimes with and sometimes without a comma separating it. Examples, with the fragments italicized:

WRONG: Feel free to talk with your date. *Because if she likes your conversation she'll give you another date.*

RIGHT:   Feel free to talk with your date, because if she likes your conversation she'll give you another date.

WRONG: Parents must let their children know that they love and trust them. *Since children who do not feel secure become behavior problems.*

RIGHT:   Parents must let their children know that they love and trust them, since children who do not feel secure become behavior problems.

WRONG: The scoutmaster and advanced scouts went exploring. *While we tenderfeet stayed at camp to gather firewood.*

RIGHT:   The scoutmaster and advanced scouts went exploring while we tenderfeet stayed at camp to gather firewood.

Subordinating connectives such as *because, since,* and *while* prevent detached dependent clauses from standing as sentences.

# 2B   DETACHED PHRASES AS SENTENCE FRAGMENTS

**Write in complete sentences; do not let a phrase stand as a sentence.**

A construction without a subject-predicate combination—that is, a phrase rather than a clause—is a fragment even if it is not introduced by a subordinating connective. Such **detached phrases** are a common source of sentence fragments. Examples, with the detached phrases italicized:

WRONG: The horse lifts his head. _His ears straight up._
RIGHT: The horse lifts his head, his ears straight up.

WRONG: The government has many people on welfare who could work. _Instead of doing nothing._
RIGHT: The government has many people on welfare who could work instead of doing nothing.

WRONG: If poor children do not have the things they need, they are likely to grow up evil. _Thus becoming problem adults._
RIGHT: If poor children do not have the things they need, they are likely to grow up evil, thus becoming problem adults.

Noun, prepositional, and verbal phrases frequently are detached from the sentences they belong to, thus becoming sentence fragments. Detached clauses and phrases are usually due to the writer's lack of sentence sense.

## 2C   SENTENCE FRAGMENTS DUE TO CONFUSED STRUCTURE

**Write in complete sentences; avoid jumbled structures.**

A third, but less common, kind of sentence fragment is one in which a necessary part of a sentence has been omitted or in which the sentence structure is jumbled rather than complete. Examples:

WRONG: Most teenagers who run away because their parents won't listen, which is the main reason for running away.
RIGHT: Most teenagers who run away because their parents won't listen, which is the main reason for running away, eventually return to try again to achieve a good home life.

WRONG: Parents, who should let their children go out and see the world, but they don't trust the children.
RIGHT: Parents should let their children go out and see the world, but they don't trust the children.

In the first example, the writer forgot to compose a predicate that would finish the sentence. In the second, the writer also forgot to provide a predicate for the subject *parents* and instead let the sentence become a jumbled fragment. Such fragments are often due to the writer's carelessness.

## 2D FRAGMENTS WITH NONFINITE VERB FORMS

**Write in complete sentences; do not let a construction with a nonfinite verb form stand as a sentence.**

A fourth, but not very common, type of sentence fragment is a construction with a **nonfinite verb form** rather than a finite (sentence-forming) verb form. Examples, with the nonfinite verb forms italicized:

WRONG:  I finished that task and then *coming* home and *sitting* down to work.

RIGHT:  I finished that task and then came home and sat down to work.

WRONG:  He *should picking* a good time to ask her for a date, so that most likely she would say yes.

RIGHT:  He should pick a good time to ask her for a date so that most likely she would say yes.

Many, perhaps most, such fragments are due to carelessness, but some are due to the writer's lack of sentence sense.

# Comma Splices and Run-Together Sentences

Independent clauses are in effect simple sentences, and two of them (perhaps with other constituents) are very often joined to form compound or compound-complex sentences. But when two independent clauses have *only* a comma and *no coordinating conjunction (and, but, yet, or, nor, so, for)* between them, a **comma splice** is formed, usually indicating that the writer has imperfect sentence sense. Without a coordinating conjunction between independent clauses, either a semicolon or a period between them is required. (A semicolon has the same force as a period, but is normally used only when the independent clauses are especially closely related.) If a period is the best mark of punctuation to use, then the second sentence of course begins with a capital letter.

# 3A   COMMA SPLICES WITHOUT CONNECTIVE WORDS

**Do not use a comma to separate two independent clauses that are not joined by a coordinating conjunction.**

Many times a comma only, with no connective, is placed between sentences (or independent clauses), thus incorrectly "splicing" the sentences and producing a **comma splice.** In such cases, the second sentence usually begins with some kind of word—such as *this, another, there, it,* and other pronouns—that leads the writer to believe that the sentence is continuing, when actually a new sentence has begun. Either a period or, occasionally, a semicolon must replace the comma to eliminate the comma splice. Examples:

WRONG:   The truly Christian person acts morally as well as attends church, this kind of behavior in everyday affairs is what the Christian religion is all about.

RIGHT:   The truly Christian person acts morally as well as attends church. This kind of behavior in everyday affairs is what the Christian religion is all about.

WRONG:   One reason an eighteen-year-old man in our state should be able to buy alcohol is that he is old enough to fight for his country, another is that he can now vote and participate in other adult affairs.

RIGHT:   One reason an eighteen-year-old man in our state should be able to buy alcohol is that he is old enough to fight for his country. Another is that he can now vote and participate in other adult affairs.

WRONG:   Why should a person be put in jail because of a few minor mistakes, there must be a better way to handle victimless crimes.

RIGHT:   Why should a person be put in jail because of a few minor mistakes? There must be a better way to handle victimless crimes.

WRONG:   Little children should be praised when they behave well, this makes them want to continue to behave well.

RIGHT:    Little children should be praised when they behave well**;**
          this makes them want to continue to behave well.

In the last example a period instead of a semicolon would also be correct. A semicolon calls for the same duration of voice pause that a period does. Thus where a period at the end of a sentence is correct, a semicolon normally cannot be called wrong, though it may produce awkward style.

# 3B  COMMA SPLICES WITH CONJUNCTIVE ADVERBS

**Do not use a comma to separate two independent clauses joined by a conjunctive adverb.**

The conjunctive adverbs — *however, therefore, nevertheless,* and so on — are coordinating connectives frequently used to join sentences (or independent clauses), but they are not coordinating conjunctions. When a comma (instead of a period or semicolon) is used with them between sentences, a comma splice occurs. Example:

WRONG: Students deserve to have a Fairness Committee set up on this campus**,** however, I admit that most student complaints about teachers are not justified.

RIGHT:    Students deserve to have a Fairness Committee set up on this campus**;** however, I admit that most student complaints about teachers are not justified.

Note several points here: (1) With a comma before and after *however,* the rapid reader might not at first know which clause the *however* goes with; quite often sentences end with a conjunctive adverb. (2) A period rather than a semicolon after *campus* would also be correct. And (3) the *however* could be shifted to the interior of the second clause, for example, after *admit.* Most of the conjunctive adverbs can be shifted to the interior of the second clause, and this fact provides you with a test for proper punctuation: if the connective can be shifted, a period or semicolon must come after the first clause.

Another example:

WRONG: Communication between parents and children is a two-
way affair, therefore, children should make an effort to
understand their parents, as well as the other way around.
RIGHT: Communication between parents and children is a two-
way affair. Therefore, children should make an effort to
understand their parents, as well as the other way around.

A semicolon after *affair* would not be wrong. The *therefore*
could be shifted, as in *Children, therefore, should . . . .*
One more example:

WRONG: I got my rifle in readiness to fire instantly, then a jackrabbit jumped from right under my nose.
RIGHT: I got my rifle in readiness to fire instantly; then a jackrabbit jumped from right under my nose.

In this sentence *then* is a conjunctive adverb, not a coordinating conjunction; thus either a semicolon or a period
must come after *instantly*. The *then* could be shifted to
come after *jackrabbit,* but that structure might sound awkward. Nevertheless, that shift is a test that shows the neces-
sity of a semicolon or period between the clauses.

# 3C    RUN-TOGETHER SENTENCES

**Do not run two sentences together with no punctuation
between them and no capital letter beginning the second
sentence.**

The error known as **run-together sentences** means that two
sentences are run together with no punctuation or coordinating conjunction between them and no capital letter
starting the second sentence. This error generally occurs
when the second sentence starts with a word such as *this,
another, there, it,* or some other pronoun, which sometimes
leads the writer to believe he or she is continuing a sentence, not starting a new one. Examples:

WRONG: After college I expect to be a law-enforcement officer that is what I have dreamed of since I was a child.

RIGHT: After college I expect to be a law-enforcement officer. That is what I have dreamed of since I was a child.

WRONG: You can also learn what you want to do with your life this is a very important aspect of a college career.

RIGHT: You can also learn what you want to do with your life. This is a very important aspect of a college career.

In such run-together sentences the fact that the second sentence does not begin with a capital letter usually indicates that the writer has not been careless but lacks full sentence sense. Semicolons could be used instead of periods between such independent clauses, but periods are usually better.

If you find that you must refer to this chapter often, you probably need to study Sections 1B and 1D carefully and perhaps need to study all of Chapter 1.

# Misused Modifiers

A **modifier** is a word or word group that describes, limits, or adds to another word or word group. The common misuses of modifiers are the incorrect use of an adjective for an adverb to modify a verb and the incorrect use of an adverb as a predicate adjective.

## 4A  MISUSED ADJECTIVE FORMS

**Do not use an adjective form to modify an intransitive or transitive verb.**

Such a misused adjective form almost always follows the verb it modifies. To determine whether a word is modifying a verb, remember that asking *what goes with what* is a useful test. For example, consider the sentence—

Jack comes to our nightly big bashes very seldom.

Ask "What does *seldom* go with?" and your answer should be *seldom comes,* showing that *seldom* modifies (goes with) the verb of the sentence.

Here are examples of adjectives misused for adverbs, with the modified verb underlined:

WRONG:  After my father inherited some money, he began to gamble *considerable.*

RIGHT:   After my father inherited some money, he began to gamble **considerably.**

WRONG:  At first I was nervous on my first date, but he talked very *friendly* and that put me at my ease.

RIGHT:   At first I was nervous on my first date, but he talked **in a friendly way** and that put me at my ease.

In the first example the *ly* adverb form *considerably* is needed to modify the verb *to gamble.* In the second example *friendly* is one of a few adjectives (*heavenly, lovely,* and others) that end in *ly* but that almost never function as adverbs. Since the adverb form *friendlily* sounds awkward, the adverbial prepositional phrase *in a friendly way* is needed to modify the verb *talked.*

Two other examples:

WRONG:  You explain it all so *clear* that I am learning more English than ever before.

RIGHT:   You explain it all so **clearly** that I am learning more English than ever before.

WRONG:  After we worked on him for some time, he began to breathe *normal* again.

RIGHT:   After we worked on him for some time, he began to breathe **normally** again.

WRONG:  Len seems to speak *different* now.

RIGHT:   Len seems to speak **differently** now.

The adverb forms *clearly* and *normally* are needed to modify the verbs *explain* and *to breathe.*

A particularly sticky writing problem involves *well,* which is both an adjective and an adverb, and *good,* which is only an adjective. A writer should always use *well* to modify a verb. Here are examples, with the verbs underlined:

WRONG:   I worked all day overhauling my bike and by evening had it <u>running</u> *good.*

RIGHT:   I worked all day overhauling my bike and by evening had it <u>running</u> **well.**

WRONG:   I went out of the exam thinking I <u>had done</u> *good.*

RIGHT:   I went out of the exam thinking I <u>had done</u> **well.**

The italicized words modify the verbs *running* and *had done,* and thus the adverb *well,* not the adjective *good,* is required. Remember that you *do well, write well, play well, argue well, dress well, behave well, work well,* and so on. (You can *feel good* or *feel well,* with somewhat different meanings.)

Another adjective form sometimes misused for an adverb is *near* for *nearly.* Examples:

WRONG:   My paper wasn't *near* as bad as your red marks made it seem.

RIGHT:   My paper wasn't **nearly** as bad as your red marks made it seem.

WRONG:   But my father, in spite of what he said, wasn't *near* as mad as my mother.

RIGHT:   But my father, in spite of what he said, wasn't **nearly** as mad as my mother.

Remember that the correct phrase is *not nearly as. . . .*

## 4B   MISUSED ADVERB FORMS

**Do not use an adverb to function as a predicate adjective after a linking verb.**

After a linking verb, the correct modifier is an adjective, which describes the subject, not an adverb. The chief linking verbs are *to be, to get, to feel, to seem, to sound, to taste, to look, to remain, to become, to appear,* and a few others; but some verbs that are normally linking — such as *to feel* and *to look* — are sometimes used as intransitive or transitive verbs. It is not possible to give a complete list of linking verbs, although there are comparatively few of them, for many normally intransitive or transitive verbs occasionally function as linking. The clue is that the linking verb is followed by an adjective that modifies the subject or by a predicate noun that renames the subject. Thus such verbs as *to go, to turn, to marry, to die, to retire,* and others are normally intransitive or transitive but occasionally function as linking, being followed by predicate adjectives that describe the subjects. Examples:

> The well went **dry.**
> Billy turned **hostile.**
> Louise married **young.**
> Dave died **old.**
> Fred retired **happy.**

Since the meanings are *dry well, hostile Billy, young Louise, old Dave,* and *happy Fred,* the verbs in these instances are linking.

The most commonly misused adverb form is *badly* after the linking verb *to feel.* Examples:

WRONG: After I was caught plagiarizing, I felt very *badly.*
RIGHT:  After I was caught plagiarizing, I felt very **bad.**

WRONG: When I began to see what grownups do, I didn't feel so *badly* about having shoplifted when I was in my early teens.
RIGHT:  When I began to see what grownups do, I didn't feel so **bad** about having shoplifted when I was in my early teens.

WRONG: I felt *badly* when I realized how I had hurt my parents.
RIGHT:  I felt **bad** when I realized how I had hurt my parents.

In these cases *feel* and *felt* are linking verbs, and therefore the adjective *bad* is needed as a predicate adjective to modify the subject *I.* Technically, *to feel badly* would mean to have a faulty sense of touch, such as being unable to tell whether a surface is smooth or rough. Also note that you would be very unlikely to say either of the following sentences:

> WRONG: I feel *sadly* about your divorce.
> WRONG: I feel *gladly* that you made an A.

*Sad* and *glad.* are clearly the correct predicate adjective forms, as is *bad.*

Occasionally a writer will incorrectly use other adverb forms with linking verbs, probably because of having heard the incorrect *I feel badly* construction. Examples:

> WRONG: We had to make a forced march at night in the rain, and we all felt as *miserably* as could be.
> RIGHT: We had to make a forced march at night in the rain, and we all felt as **miserable** as could be.

> WRONG: When I was a child I stole a watermelon from a patch, and I still remember how *unpleasantly* it tasted, because I was so scared.
> RIGHT: When I was a child I stole a watermelon from a patch, and I still remember how **unpleasant** it tasted, because I was so scared.

*Miserable* and *unpleasant* are needed as predicate adjectives to go with the linking verbs *felt* and *tasted* and to modify the subjects *we* and *it.* In the last example, the predicate adjective precedes its linking verb and subject. This is not an especially common construction but is not rare, either.

# 4C   DOUBLE NEGATIVES

### Do not use a double negative.

A **double negative** is a construction in which two words expressing negation—such as *no* and *nothing*—are used to make one negative statement. In usage, such constructions are considered in the same unacceptable category as *ain't.* Examples, with the two negative words italicized:

WRONG: But after walking the streets for hours I could *not* make *no* sales of that soap.

RIGHT:   But after walking the streets for hours I could **not** make **any** sales of that soap.

WRONG: It did*n't* mean *nothing* to us to lose that game, since we had the title cinched.

RIGHT:   It did**n't** mean **anything** to us to lose that game, since we had the title cinched.

Remember that the correct constructions are *not . . . any, not . . . anything, not . . . anyone,* and *don't (doesn't) . . . any* (rather than *no*).

Another incorrect double negative involves the words *hardly* and *scarcely.* Since these words are both negatives, using another negative in a construction with one of them produces a double negative. Examples, with the double negatives italicized:

WRONG: Some parents do*n't* pay *hardly* any attention to their children as soon as they are old enough to play outside.

RIGHT:   Some parents pay **hardly any** attention to their children as soon as they are old enough to play outside.

WRONG: It had*n't scarcely* begun to rain before the floor of our tent was flooded.

RIGHT:   It **had scarcely** begun to rain before the floor of our tent was flooded.

Remember never to use *no* or *not* in a construction with *hardly* or *scarcely.*

# Pronoun Case Forms

**Case** is the grammatical function that requires (though not in all instances) the change of the form of a pronoun according to its use in a sentence. The **subjective case** forms — *I, we, she,* and so on — are used as subjects and as predicate nouns, or, more exactly, predicate pronouns. The **objective case** forms — *me, us, her,* and so on — are used as objects of verbs and prepositions. And the **possessive case** forms — *my, our, her,* and so on — are used to show possession. Sometimes writers use incorrect pronoun case forms.

## 5A IN COMPOUND CONSTRUCTIONS

**In compound constructions use subjective case forms as subjects and objective case forms as objects.**

A compound construction is one in which two or more parts are coordinated, or used in a series of two or more. Very seldom does anyone use a wrong pronoun case form when a single pronoun is a subject or object. For example, you could wait for years and probably not hear such constructions as these:

WRONG: *Me* was invited to Jane's party.
WRONG: The package was for *I.*

But often when two pronouns, or a noun and a pronoun, occur in a compound construction, a faulty pronoun case form is used.

Here are examples in compound subjects, with the faulty pronoun forms italicized:

WRONG: My dad and *me* could hardly wait for our hunting trip to begin.
RIGHT: My dad and **I** could hardly wait for our hunting trip to begin.

WRONG: The teacher and *him* got into a big argument.
RIGHT: The teacher and **he** got into a big argument.

The subjective forms *I* and *he* are needed to serve as subjects of *were* and *got.* When in doubt you can test such constructions by omitting one part of the compound construction. That is, omit *dad* and *teacher* in the above examples and you will immediately see that *me could hardly wait* and *him got into an argument* are incorrect. Remember that the correct expressions are such as these: *Melissa and she arrived, José and I conferred, the Joneses and they are . . ., the Alvarados and we began . . .,* and so on.

Similarly, subjective case forms should *not* be used in compound constructions that are objects of verbs or prepositions. Examples, with the incorrect pronoun case form italicized:

WRONG: My mother told my sister and *I* that dad was on the warpath.
RIGHT: My mother told my sister and **me** that dad was on the warpath.

WRONG: The argument was just between my sister and *I.*
RIGHT: The argument was just between my sister and **me.**

Again, a simple test is to drop one part of the compound structure (*sister* in the above examples). You would not write "My mother told I . . ." or "The argument was between I. . . ." Clearly, since the pronoun is the object of the verb *told* and of the preposition *between,* the objective form — *me* — is needed. Remember that the correct expressions are such as these: *between you and me, for Tom and him, with Jack and me, overheard Mary and her, invited the Medinas and us,* and so on.

# 5B AFTER *TO BE*

**Use subjective pronoun forms after forms of the verb to be.**

Since the verb *to be* is a linking verb, any predicate noun or pronoun that follows a form of it renames the subject. Therefore since the subject is, obviously, in the subjective case, a predicate pronoun, which is the same as the subject, should also be in the subjective case. But in informal use nowadays objective pronoun forms are usually acceptable after forms of *to be.* Examples, with the pronouns in bold-face:

INFORMAL: It's **me.**
INFORMAL: I'm sure it was **her.**
INFORMAL: Could you have been **him?**
INFORMAL: Did you think it was **us?**

However, in semiformal and formal situations subjective pronoun case forms should follow forms of *to be.* Examples:

SEMIFORMAL: It's **I.**
SEMIFORMAL: The guilty ones were **they.**
SEMIFORMAL: I'm sure it was **she.**
SEMIFORMAL: It might be **he** who wins.

Even in informal conversation many people still prefer the subjective case forms in such constructions.

# 5C WHO AND WHOM

**Use *who* (or *whoever*) in subject positions and *whom* (or *whomever*) in object positions.**

However, it is customary nowadays in informal conversation to use *who* as an object except directly after a preposition. Examples:

INFORMAL: **Who** were you talking to? (object of *to*)
INFORMAL: I don't care **who** you invite. (object of *invite*)

But in semiformal or formal writing you should distinguish between *who* and *whom*. Examples:

RIGHT: I voted for the candidate **whom** my father voted for. (object of *voted for*)
RIGHT: It got so we were always wondering **whom** the cops would bust next. (object of *would bust*)
RIGHT: You should always vote for the candidate **who** you feel will do the best job. (subject of *will do*)
RIGHT: I was ready to give the answers to **whoever** asked me for them. (subject of *asked;* the whole noun clause *whoever asked me for them* is the object of *to.*)

Sometimes you may need to test a construction in order to choose the right form of *who.* The test is this: (1) turn a question into a simple sentence or express the part of a sentence containing a form of *who* as a simple sentence; then (2) see whether *he* or *him* fits the *who* slot in your simple sentence. If *he* fits, use *who;* if *him* fits, use *whom.* Examples:

_____ did the jury say was guilty?
(Who *or* Whom?)

The jury did say *he* was guilty. (not *him*)
**Who** did the jury say was guilty?

_____ was Professor Skole angry with?
(Who *or* Whom?)

Professor Skole was angry with *him.* (not *he*)
**Whom** was Professor Skole angry with?

We usually become fonder of someone _____
  we do a favor for.                    (who *or* whom?)

We do a favor for *him*. (So use *whom* as the object of *for*, even
  though *whom* doesn't come directly after *for*.)

We usually become fonder of someone **whom** we do a favor for.

Shelley is the student _____ it seems will be
                          (who *or* whom?)
  selected to give the graduation address.

It seems *she* will be selected. (So use *who* as the subject of
  *will be selected*.)

Shelley is the student **who** it seems will be selected to give the
  graduation address.

The test is simple and reliable. We should note that even in
casual conversation some people still prefer to distinguish
between *who* and *whom*.

# 5D  IN COMPARATIVE CONSTRUCTIONS

**After the comparative words *as* and *than* use the pronoun
case form that the understood part of the clause calls for.**

In such a sentence as—

  I gave more to charity than _____,
                                (he *or* him?)

a part of a dependent clause is understood but not stated.
In the above sentence the understood part is *(than he) gave
to charity*. Testing such sentences by mentally supplying the
understood part of the clause will tell you the correct pronoun to use. Examples, with the understood parts in
parentheses:

RIGHT: My parents have always treated my sister better than (they
       treated) **me.**

RIGHT: Donna Smith deserved the award as much as **I** (deserved
       the award).

RIGHT: Bruce gave Betty more money than (he gave) **me.**

RIGHT: Bruce gave Betty more money than **I** (gave Betty).

As the last two examples show, the pronoun form at the end of a comparative construction sometimes determines the meaning. The test for choosing the correct form is both simple and reliable.

## 5E  WITH VERBAL PHRASES

**Use the possessive form of a pronoun (or noun) to modify an *ing* verbal phrase when the phrase refers to just one aspect of a person and not the person as a whole.**

Example, with the pronoun form in boldface:

RIGHT: We all agreed with Derick, but we could see that the coach was furious at **his** not having followed orders.

*Him* would be incorrect, for the coach was not furious at him as a whole but only at his not having followed orders. Two more examples:

RIGHT: Jill heard **me** coming, and she did not like **my** coming on a motorcycle.
RIGHT: We were delayed by the McCombs' arriving an hour late.

The *me* is correct because it refers to the whole person, and the *my* is correct because it refers to just one action of the person. In other words, the sentence does not say that "she did not like me" but only that she did not like one of my actions. Similarly, the possessive form *McCombs'* is correct.

## 5F  THE *WE STUDENTS-US STUDENTS* CONSTRUCTION

**Use *we* or *us* in conjunction with a noun according to whether the noun functions as a subject or object.**

If the noun is a subject, use *we;* if it is an object, use *us.* The very simple test that will guide you correctly in choosing *we* or *us* is to mentally omit the noun and then to use the pronoun form that sounds natural. Examples, with the noun to be mentally omitted in parentheses:

RIGHT: After three meetings, **we** (students) decided we did not want to sit on the Administrative Committee.
RIGHT: **We** (girls) in the dorm do not have as much freedom as those who live in town.
RIGHT: Then the coach gave **us** (players) the worst dressing down we had ever had.
RIGHT: The judge was simply unfair to **us** (demonstrators) who committed no violent acts.

Since no one would write such constructions as *us decided* or *to we,* this simple test is thoroughly reliable.

# 5G DEMONSTRATIVE PRONOUNS

**Never use *them* as a demonstrative ("pointing") pronoun in place of *these* or *those.***

Examples:

WRONG: I asked for *them* books to be reserved for me.
RIGHT:  I asked for **those** books to be reserved for me.

WRONG (pointing and speaking with emphasis): I want one of *them.*
RIGHT:  I want one of **those** (or **these**).

When there is no pointing action, *them* is correct, as in—

I was the first to see **them.**

# 5H REFLEXIVE PRONOUNS

**In semiformal or formal writing do not use a reflexive pronoun as a subject or object.**

Examples:

WRONG: Jerry and *myself* managed to slip through the transom into our dorm's kitchen.

RIGHT:    Jerry and **I** managed to slip through the transom into our
          dorm's kitchen.

WRONG:  It turned out that the invitation was for both my brother
          and *myself*.

RIGHT:    It turned out that the invitation was for both my brother and
          **me.**

An exception to this rule is the use of the reflexive pronoun
as an object when it refers to the same person as the subject, as in *I cut myself.*

Also avoid these incorrect spellings of the reflexive
pronouns: *hisself, theirselves,* and *its self.* The correct
forms are *himself, themselves,* and *itself.*

# Subject-Verb Agreement

The grammatical term **number** has to do, obviously, with the number of units involved. The two numbers in our grammar are the **singular** (one) and the **plural** (more than one). For writing to be correct, verbs must agree in number with their subjects. This writing problem is limited, however, because all English verbs except *to be* have singular and plural forms only in the present tense. And even then the only variation in verb form for number is that the third person singular, present tense verb form ends in *s* or *es*, as in *John walks*, *Shirley touches*, and so on; the other present tense form (*walk, touch,* and so on) is used with *I, you, we, they*, and plural nouns. The verb *to be* has number in the present tense *(am, is, are)* and in the past tense *(was, were)*. The auxiliaries *to have* and *to do* have number only in the present tense *(has, have* and *does, do)*. The modal auxiliaries (*can, could,* and so on) do not have number. But in spite of the limited opportunities to make errors in subject-verb agreement in English, there are a number of trouble spots, which we will cover in the following sections.

# 6A   NOUN PHRASES AS SUBJECTS

**The verb of a sentence should agree in number with the headword of a noun-phrase subject.**

Of course, many subjects are single nouns, such as a person's name. But often a noun phrase functions as a subject. The whole noun phrase is the **full subject,** and the **headword** of the noun phrase is the **simple subject.** The headword is the noun (or noun substitute, such as *many*) that governs the entire phrase; all other words and word groups in the noun phrase either modify the headword or modify other words in the phrase. The simple subject, or headword of the noun phrase, governs the verb. Thus singular headwords call for singular verbs and plural headwords call for plural verbs. Here are examples, with the headwords, or simple subjects, and the verbs in boldface:

RIGHT: A smelly **pile** of old water-soaked haystacks **was** our refuge.
RIGHT: A **man** who has a domineering wife and only daughters for children always **looks** harried.

The singular headwords (simple subjects) *pile* and *man* govern the singular verbs *was* and *looks.*

RIGHT: Several **coeds** with a lot of money but no brains **were** very popular in Las Vegas.

The plural simple subject *coeds* takes the plural verb *were.*

When the headword is followed by a prepositional phrase with the compound preposition *as well as* or *together with,* the object of the prepositional phrase does not affect the verb. Also, the prepositional phrase is often set off by commas. Examples:

WRONG: The *scoutmaster* as well as the advanced scouts *were* trying to bully us tenderfeet.
RIGHT: The **scoutmaster,** as well as the advanced scouts, **was** trying to bully us tenderfeet.

WRONG: Our club *leader,* together with three "bodyguards," *were* staked out in our tree house.

RIGHT: Our club **leader,** together with three "bodyguards," **was** staked out in our tree house.

# 6B INDEFINITE PRONOUNS AS SUBJECTS

**The indefinite pronouns *one, each, either,* and *neither* are singular and require singular verbs.**

Examples:

WRONG: *Either* of the answers *are* correct.

RIGHT: **Either** of the answers **is** correct.

RIGHT: At least **one** of the members **is** coming.

RIGHT: **Neither is** the kind I am looking for.

RIGHT: **Each** of the twins **was** surprised to be chosen.

The indefinite pronouns *any* and *none* may correctly take either a singular or a plural verb. Example:

RIGHT: **None** of you **are** (or **is**) to blame.

RIGHT: **Any** of the voters **is** (or **are**) entitled to challange the candidates.

# 6C RELATIVE PRONOUNS AS SUBJECTS

**When a relative pronoun functions as a subject, its verb agrees in number with the pronoun's antecedent.**

This means that *who, whom, which,* and *that* are either singular or plural according to the nouns they refer to. Examples, with the relative pronoun, its antecedent, and the verb in boldface:

RIGHT: I have an **uncle** in Peoria **who** still **makes** bathtub gin.

RIGHT: The **theories** of cosmogony **which** in the future **are** likely to be re-examined are the big-bang and steady-state theories.

A special subject-verb agreement problem involving relative pronouns appears in sentences with the construction *one of those* _____ *who* (or *which* or *that*). Example:

RIGHT: Steve is one of those **students who do** well in all subjects. (*Does* would be wrong.)

The point is that *students,* and not *Steve,* is the antecedent of *who,* which means that a plural verb is required. When in doubt, you can use a simple test to choose the proper verb. All such sentences as the one illustrated will undergo this transformation:

Of those **students who do** well in all subjects, Steve is one.

This test clearly shows the verb form needed.

# 6D COMPOUND SUBJECTS

Compound subjects consist of two or more coordinated constituents (or unified parts of a sentence).

### 6D1 With the Coordinating Conjunction *and*

**When two (or more) subjects are joined by *and,* they form a plural subject and should take a plural verb.**

Examples:

RIGHT: My uncle **and** one of my cousins **are** going to Las Vegas with me.
RIGHT: Where you go **and** whom you go with **are** none of my business.

But when two nouns or constructions joined by *and* are considered a single unit, they take a singular verb. Examples:

RIGHT: Apple pie and cheese **is** on the menu.
RIGHT: Some gas and dust actually **shows** up in photographs of interstellar space.

*Apple pie and cheese* is considered a single dish; *gas and dust* is considered a unified, or singular, mass of matter.

### 6D2  With Correlatives and *but not*

**When compound subjects are joined by one of the correlatives or by *but not,* the verb agrees in number with the part of the subject closest to the verb.**

The correlatives are the two-part connectives *either (neither) . . . or (nor), not only . . . but (also),* and *not . . . but.* (The correlative *both . . . and* makes compound subjects just as *and* by itself does.) Examples, with the noun governing the verb and the verb in boldface:

RIGHT: Either a wolf or small **dogs were** responsible for the kill.
RIGHT: Either small dogs or a **wolf was** responsible for the kill.

RIGHT: Not only a police sergeant but two **plainclothesmen are** assigned to this case.
RIGHT: Not only two plainclothesmen but also a police **sergeant is** assigned to this case.

RIGHT: Not a boy but several **girls are** the guilty ones.
RIGHT: Not those girls but a **boy is** the guilty one.

Sometimes the *either* of *either . . . or* and the *also* of *not only . . . but also* are omitted, but the rule for subject-verb agreement stays the same.
    When two subjects are joined by the connective *but not,* the verb agrees in number with the part of the subject closest to the verb. Examples:

RIGHT: All the wives but not a single **husband was** willing to go.
RIGHT: Mr. Busbee but not his **children were** willing to go.

# 6E  SPECIAL NOUNS AS SUBJECTS

Three special kinds of nouns sometimes cause problems in subject-verb agreement.

## 6E1   Collective Nouns

**Collective nouns take singular verbs unless they are used so as to mean individuals and not a group.**

Collective nouns are those singular in form but plural in meaning, since they specify many individuals. Some of the most common collective nouns are *family, team, crew, series, jury, flock, student body, faculty, staff, pride* (of lions), *gaggle* (of geese), *collection,* and so on. Examples:

RIGHT: The English **staff is** holding a meeting.
RIGHT: The **jury is** deadlocked.
RIGHT: The **team is** in excellent physical shape.

When a collective noun is used so that it must be thought of as meaning separate individuals, then it takes a plural verb. Example:

RIGHT: My family **are** individualists.

Such use of collective nouns is not common.

The collective nouns *number, crowd, group,* and perhaps a few others pose a different problem. When one of these singular nouns is followed by a prepositional phrase with a plural noun object, the verb may be plural. Examples, with the simple subjects and the verbs in boldface:

RIGHT: A **number** of students **were** suspended.
RIGHT: A **crowd** of spectators **were** injured.
RIGHT: A **group** of Mohawks **were** on the prowl.

Some writers prefer singular verbs in such sentences, and that usage is of course correct. But individuals are so clearly meant in the example sentences and others like them that the plural verb must also be considered correct. Some experts prefer the plural verb.

## 6E2   Singular Nouns Plural in Form

**Normally, nouns plural in form but singular in meaning take singular verbs.**

The most common such nouns are *economics, physics, mathematics, politics, statistics, checkers, measles, mumps,* and *molasses.* Examples:

RIGHT: Physics **is** my hardest course.
RIGHT: Politics **is** a risky profession.
RIGHT: Measles **is** a serious disease.
RIGHT: Checkers **is** an intellectual game.

### 6E3   Nouns of Weight, Measurement, Time, and Money

**A plural noun that establishes a weight or measurement or a period of time or an amount of money takes a singular verb.**

Examples:

RIGHT: Two hundred and fifty pounds **is** not an unusual weight for a football player.
RIGHT: Five miles **is** a long distance to walk.
RIGHT: Two years **is** the gestation period for elephants.
RIGHT: Forty dollars **is** the least I will take for that record.

# 6F   SUBJECTS IN INVERTED SENTENCE ORDER

**When a subject follows its verb, the verb still agrees in number with the subject.**

Examples, with the verbs and subjects in boldface:

RIGHT: Standing at the professor's lectern **were** two **chimpanzees.**
RIGHT: Under the rose bushes **is** a stretched-out **king snake.**

Note that the nouns *lectern* and *bushes* have no effect on the verbs.

The most common kind of inverted sentence order, however, and the one that gives most trouble in subject-verb agreement, is the sentence that begins with *there* and has its subject following the verb. The *there* is just a filler and has no meaning. The verb agrees with the subject. Examples:

WRONG: There *is* some *parents* who just won't give their children a chance to talk to them.

RIGHT: There **are** some **parents** who just won't give their children a chance to talk to them.

WRONG: There *exists* many *ways* that students use to cheat on exams.

RIGHT: There **exist** many **ways** that students use to cheat on exams.

When the opening word *there* does not mean a place, the sentence subject will follow its verb.

# Shifts

Various kinds of inconsistencies frequently occur in writing because of **faulty shifts in grammatical constructions.** That is, a writer will begin with one kind of grammatical construction but will unnecessarily (and incorrectly) shift to a different kind of construction. Example:

INCONSISTENT: The American child is different from his European counterparts.

This writer opened with the singular *American child,* thus committing himself (or herself) to talking about children in general in the singular, which is perfectly acceptable. But then he inconsistently shifted to the plural *European counterparts.* The writer either should have continued in the singular with *European counterpart* or should have begun with the plural *American children.* Maintaining complete grammatical consistency is not an easy task even for professional writers. In this chapter we will deal briefly and simply with the six kinds of shifts that produce most inconsistencies. These are shifts in **number, person, tense, voice, mood,** and **point of view.**

# 7A IN NUMBER

**Do not inconsistently shift from the singular to the plural or from the plural to the singular.**

The most common kind of faulty shift in number is from a singular noun to a plural pronoun. Examples:

INCONSISTENT: The *teacher* always thinks *they are* right because *they don't* want to admit that *they know* less than a student.

CONSISTENT: **Teachers** always think **they are** right because **they don't** want to admit that **they know** less than a student.

INCONSISTENT: I think that a college *athlete* should be paid, because *they work* just as hard as teachers do.

CONSISTENT: I think that college **athletes** should be paid, because **they work** just as hard as teachers do.

Sometimes, however, the faulty shift is from the plural to the singular. Example:

INCONSISTENT: *People* are honest most of the time only because *one doesn't* like *one's* neighbors to know that *he* or *she is* a cheater.

CONSISTENT: **People are** honest most of the time only because **they don't** like **their** neighbors to know that **they are** cheaters.

You must give thought to whether you will write in the singular or the plural in order to avoid such shifts.

# 7B IN PERSON

**Do not inconsistently shift from the third person to the second or from the second person to the third.**

There are three **persons** in English grammar: (1) the **first person** is the person speaking *(I, me, we, us);* (2) the **second person** is the person spoken to *(you);* and (3) the **third person** is the person or thing spoken about *(he, him, she, her, it, they, them,* and all nouns and indefinite pronouns). The grammatical inconsistency dealt with in this section is due to our language's use of the **indefinite second person** *you* to refer to people in general. Use of the indefinite *you* is not at all improper, but it is improper to begin a passage in the third person and then to shift inconsistently to the indefinite *you.* Examples:

INCONSISTENT: College is designed to aid *those* interested in becoming educated. Without the opportunity to attend college, *you* might not receive the education *you* will need in *your* vocation.

CONSISTENT: College is designed to aid **those** interested in becoming educated. Without the opportunity to attend college, **one** might not receive the education **he** or **she** will need in a vocation.

INCONSISTENT: Most parents constantly strive to give their *children* a sense of security. If *you* grow up feeling insecure, *your* parents have failed *you.*

CONSISTENT: Most parents constantly strive to give their **children** a sense of security. If **children** grow up feeling insecure, **their** parents have failed **them.**

Note particularly in the first example the use of the indefinite third person pronoun *one* to maintain consistency in person. Very many of the improper shifts from the third person to the indefinite *you* are due to the writer's failure to understand the use of the third person *one,* which refers to people in general.

# 7C  IN TENSE

**In summarizing fiction or history, do not inconsistently shift from the past to the present tense or the present to the past tense.**

There are a number of different present and past tenses, but we need not differentiate among them; just recognizing that a verb is in one of the present or one of the past tenses is enough. In summarizing events of the past we may use either the past tense or the **historical present tense,** but the writer who inconsistently shifts from one to the other is careless. Examples:

INCONSISTENT: In the story a boy named Giovanni *had gone* to Padua to study. He *rents* a room and from it he *looks* into a very weird garden.

CONSISTENT: In the story a boy named Giovanni **has gone** to Padua to study. He **rents** a room and from it he **looks** into a very weird garden.

INCONSISTENT: In the 1932 election campaign FDR *promised* to reduce taxes if he *was elected*. But in 1933 he *begins* to ask Congress for tax increases and *continues* to ask for increases every year.

CONSISTENT: In the 1932 election campaign FDR **promised** to reduce taxes if he **was elected.** But in 1933 he **began** to ask Congress for tax increases and **continued** to ask for them every year.

In each of these examples the writer began a summary in the past tense and inconsistently shifted to the historical present. In the first example we restored consistency by changing the past tense *(had gone)* to the present *(has gone).* In the second, we changed the present tense *(begins, continues)* to the past *(began, continued).* The point is to be consistent. You should *know* which tense you have chosen for a summary and should stick to it.

# 7D IN VOICE

**Do not inconsistently shift from the active to the passive voice.**

In the active voice, the subject performs the action; in the passive voice the subject receives the action. Sometimes there are good reasons for using the active voice and sometimes there are good reasons for using the passive. But once you have started describing a sequence of actions in the active voice, do not inconsistently shift to the passive.

(If you shift from the passive to the active, you should have started in the active voice to begin with.) Example:

INCONSISTENT: I first *place* the bit in the horse's mouth and *adjust* the bridle. Then the saddle blanket and saddle *are put* on. Now I *am* ready to mount.

CONSISTENT: I first **place** the bit in the horse's mouth and **adjust** the bridle. Then I **put** the saddle blanket and saddle on. Now I **am** ready to mount.

In the inconsistent passage, the first and third sentences are properly in the active voice, but the middle sentence is inconsistently in the passive voice. Since the writer is performing all the actions, there is no reason to say vaguely that they are performed.

# 7E   IN MOOD

**Do not inconsistently shift from the imperative to the subjunctive mood.**

Verbs have mood. Request or command sentences are in the imperative mood, which is also often used for giving directions. That is, you might say to someone—

First **go** to . . . . Then **take** the first left . . . . After that, **turn** at . . . .

The boldface verbs are in the imperative mood, directly telling someone to do certain things. One form of the subjunctive mood uses the modal auxiliaries *should* and *ought to* so that the writer does not tell someone to do something but rather that he or she *should* do something. In giving directions, do not inconsistently shift from the imperative to the subjunctive mood. Example:

INCONSISTENT: The first thing to do in breaking a wild mustang stallion is not to let him get close enough to kick or bite you. *Keep* him tethered and hobbled for the first few days. *Feed* him by placing grain under his head and leaving him to himself for a while. Next you *should try* just to touch him gently. After you have got him used to your presence, you *should try* getting a bridle on him, without a bit. When you do try getting the bit into his mouth, *keep* him hobbled and *keep* his head in a tight grasp so that he can't bite you.

CONSISTENT:  (Simply remove the *you should*'s from sentences four and five.)

It is possible, of course, to give directions so that *essential* steps are phrased in the imperative mood and *desirable* (but not essential) steps are phrased in the subjunctive mood, but no such differentiation exists in the passage above. To be consistent, such a passage requires *keep, feed, try,* and other such verbs in the imperative mood.

# 7F **IN POINT OF VIEW**

**Do not inconsistently shift the point of view when discussing or explaining someone's opinions.**

*Point of view* refers to the source of an opinion or idea being presented. The writing should make clear whether the opinion is the writer's own or that of someone being discussed. Sentences should be composed so that the point of view does not inconsistently shift. Example:

INCONSISTENT:  Everybody nowadays thinks slavery is a wholly inhumane and unacceptable institution, but Aristotle thought it was rooted in human nature and thus acceptable. Some people are born to be leaders and some to be followers or servants. Human nature can't be changed, and thus the slave class remains the slave class. Slavery is fixed in human nature.

CONSISTENT:  Everybody nowadays thinks slavery is a wholly inhumane and unacceptable institution, but Aristotle thought that it was rooted in human nature and thus acceptable. **He claimed** that some people are born to be leaders and some to be followers or servants. **He maintained** that human nature can't be changed and that that is why the slave class remains the slave class. Slavery, **he argued,** is fixed in human nature.

In the inconsistent passage the writer began by stating a modern point of view and contrasting it with Aristotle's. But the passage fails to show that the last three sentences reflect Aristotle's point of view also. In the consistent passage, the *he claimed, he maintained,* and *he argued* clearly retain Aristotle's point of view and prevent inconsistency.

# Verb Forms

Incorrect subject-verb agreement (Chapter 6) perhaps accounts for most verb problems in writing. However, occasionally wrong verb forms are used, chiefly because English has both regular and irregular verbs that sometimes cause confusion. All English verbs (with slight exceptions for *to be*) have five forms, as follows:

| *infinitive* | *third-person singular, present tense* | *present participle* | *past tense* | *past participle* |
|---|---|---|---|---|
| to talk | talks | talking | talked | talked |
| to freeze | freezes | freezing | froze | frozen |
| to bring | brings | bringing | brought | brought |

The present tense (except for the third person) is always the infinitive without the *to*. The first three forms of all verbs are regular; differences in some verbs appear in the last two forms. Verbs that end in *ed* in the past tense and past participle are called **regular;** others are **irregular,** sometimes with the past tense and past participle being different from each other (as with *freeze*) and sometimes identical (as with *bring*).

For your reference, here is a list of the so-called **principal parts** of the chief irregular verbs in English. The stem is the present tense, or the infinitive without the *to.*

| *stem* | *past tense* | *past participle* |
|---|---|---|
| arise | arose | has arisen |
| bear | bore | has borne, was born |
| begin | began | has begun |
| bind | bound | has bound |
| blow | blew | has blown |
| break | broke | has broken |
| bring | brought | has brought |
| buy | bought | has bought |
| catch | caught | has caught |
| choose | chose | has chosen |
| come | came | has come |
| creep | crept | has crept |
| deal | dealt | has dealt |
| dive | dived, dove | has dived |
| do | did | has done |
| draw | drew | has drawn |
| drink | drank | has drunk |
| drive | drove | has driven |
| eat | ate | has eaten |
| fall | fell | has fallen |
| flee | fled | has fled |
| fly | flew | has flown |
| forbid | forbad, forbade | has forbidden |
| freeze | froze | has frozen |
| give | gave | has given |
| go | went | has gone |
| grow | grew | has grown |

# VERB FORMS

| stem | past tense | past participle |
|------|-----------|-----------------|
| hang | hung | has hung |
| hang (execution) | hanged | has hanged |
| know | knew | has known |
| lay | laid | has laid |
| lead | led | has led |
| lie | lay | has lain |
| lose | lost | has lost |
| mean | meant | has meant |
| ride | rode | has ridden |
| ring | rang | has rung |
| rise | rose | has risen |
| run | ran | has run |
| see | saw | has seen |
| seek | sought | has sought |
| send | sent | has sent |
| shake | shook | has shaken |
| shine | shone, shined | has shone, has shined |
| sing | sang | has sung |
| sleep | slept | has slept |
| speak | spoke | has spoken |
| spin | spun | has spun |
| spit | spat | has spat |
| spread | spread | has spread |
| steal | stole | has stolen |
| stink | stank | has stunk |
| swear | swore | has sworn |
| swim | swam | has swum |
| swing | swung | has swung |
| take | took | has taken |
| teach | taught | has taught |
| tear | tore | has torn |
| thrive | thrived, throve | has thrived, thriven |
| throw | threw | has thrown |
| wear | wore | has worn |
| weep | wept | has wept |
| write | wrote | has written |

# 8A  PAST-TENSE FORMS

**Do not use the past participle of an irregular verb as the past-tense form, unless the two are identical.**

Examples:

WRONG: When my parents *begun* to pressure me about my school work, I did even worse.

RIGHT: When my parents **began** to pressure me about my school work, I did even worse.

WRONG: I *swum* forty laps in record time.

RIGHT: I **swam** forty laps in record time.

WRONG: We *drunk* more than three cases that night at Hollis's apartment.

RIGHT: We **drank** more than three cases that night at Hollis's apartment.

# 8B  PAST-PARTICIPLE FORMS; *COULD OF*

**Do not use the past-tense form of an irregular verb as the past participle, unless the two are identical.**

The past participle is always used with an auxiliary, often *has, have,* or *had* (see list above). Examples:

WRONG: I *had chose* the wrong course in math, and consequently I failed.

RIGHT: I **had chosen** the wrong course in math, and consequently I failed.

WRONG: After we *had began* our last practice session, word came that Fresno was dropping out of the tournament.

RIGHT: After we **had begun** our last practice session, word came that Fresno was dropping out of the tournament.

WRONG: I *had ran* the hundred-yard dash in ten seconds and still came in third.

RIGHT: I **had run** the hundred-yard dash in ten seconds and still came in third.

**Also, do not convert an irregular verb form into an incorrect regular form.**

Examples:

WRONG: The wind *blowed* all the time we were in Las Vegas.
RIGHT: The wind **blew** all the time we were in Las Vegas.

WRONG: If I *had knowed* about the importance of English, I might have studied more when I was here the first time.
RIGHT: If I **had known** about the importance of English, I might have studied more when I was here the first time.

**Never use the word *of* for the contraction of *have*.**

The two forms sound the same and thus the error is common. Example:

WRONG: I *could of* made the team if I had tried harder.
RIGHT: I **could've (could have)** made the team if I had tried harder.

# 8C TO LIE—TO LAY; TO SIT—TO SET; TO BEAR

**Do not confuse *lay* with *lie* or *set* with *sit*.**

Here are the principal parts of these verbs:

| *present tense* | *present participle* | *past tense* | *past participle* |
|---|---|---|---|
| lie, lies (to recline) | lying | lay | lain |
| lay, lays (to place or put) | laying | laid | laid |
| sit, sits (to be seated) | sitting | sat | sat |
| set, sets (to place something) | setting | set | set |

*To lie* is an intransitive verb; virtually no one ever uses it incorrectly, that is, as a transitive verb (as in the incorrect *I will lie the book down*). Examples of its use:

RIGHT: I **lie** down when I have a headache.
RIGHT: I **lay** on the floor for hours before anyone found me.
RIGHT: I **had lain** in bed longer than usual.
RIGHT: I **had been lying** in the muck for some time.

*To lay* is a transitive verb and is used correctly only when it has a direct object. Examples, with the verbs and direct objects in boldface:

RIGHT: I **lay** my **gun** down whenever I hear other hunters.
RIGHT: I **laid** the **bottle** of wine slightly up-ended.
RIGHT: I **have laid** expensive **carpet** professionally for a year.
RIGHT: I **was laying** the **baby** down when the phone rang.

The errors come when forms of *lay* are used instead of forms of *lie.* Examples:

WRONG: I need to *lay* down.
RIGHT:  I need to **lie** down.

WRONG: I *laid* in bed all morning.
RIGHT:  I **lay** in bed all morning.

WRONG: I *had laid* under the rose bushes for an hour.
RIGHT:  I **had lain** under the rose bushes for an hour.

WRONG: I *was laying* in ambush.
RIGHT:  I **was lying** in ambush.

*To sit* is also an intransitive verb. Virtually no one ever uses it incorrectly, that is, as a transitive verb (as in the incorrect *I'll sit the table*). Examples of its use:

RIGHT: That empty bottle **sits** on the mantel as a symbol.
RIGHT: Another bottle **sat** there last year.
RIGHT: I **have sat** on antique chairs before.
RIGHT: Joe **has been sitting** in front of the TV for twelve hours.

*To set* is a transitive verb used correctly (except for some uncommon meanings) only when it has a direct object. Examples, with the verbs and direct objects in boldface:

RIGHT: I **will set** the **bottle** down immediately.
RIGHT: Yesterday I **set it** in a hiding place.
RIGHT: I **have set** potted **plants** all around the house.
RIGHT: I **was setting** the **plants** in their tubs when Mavis arrived.

The errors come when forms of *set* are used instead of forms of *sit.* Examples:

WRONG: Let's *set* for a spell.
RIGHT:  Let's **sit** for a spell.

WRONG: Donny just *set* in his seat like a goon.
RIGHT:  Donny just **sat** in his seat like a goon.

WRONG: *Has* Charlie *set* there all day?
RIGHT: **Has** Charlie **sat** there all day?

WRONG: We *were* just *setting* around talking.
RIGHT: We **were** just **sitting** around talking.

The verb *to bear* also needs mentioning. In active-voice sentences, its past participle is *borne.* Examples:

RIGHT: Elaine **has borne** six children.
RIGHT: I **have borne** all the slander I can take.

But in the passive voice, *born* is the past participle of *to bear* in the meaning of coming into the world. Example:

RIGHT: I **was born** in Muncie, Indiana.

# 8D SUBJUNCTIVE VERB FORMS

**Do not use the indicative form of a verb when a subjunctive form is needed.**

The indicative mood states facts or what are thought to be facts. The subjunctive mood states conditions contrary to fact or conveys desirability or urgency of some sort. In informal speech the indicative mood is often used for conditions contrary to fact, and so on, but in semiformal speech and writing the subjunctive mood is preferred. Examples:

INFORMAL:     I wish I *was* my own boss.
SEMIFORMAL: I wish I **were** my own boss.

WRONG: We desire that this application form *is* filled out in triplicate.
RIGHT:   We desire that this application form **be** filled out in triplicate.

WRONG: It is obligatory that he *is* an eagle scout.
RIGHT:   It is obligatory that he **be** an eagle scout.

WRONG: We demand that she *comes* immediately.
RIGHT:   We demand that she **come** immediately.

# SECTION TWO

# PUNCTUATION AND MECHANICS

# 9

# End Punctuation

End punctuation occurs at the end of sentences and of some constructions that are not sentences.

## 9A THE PERIOD

**Use a period to end a normal sentence that is not a question and is not especially emphatic.**

Declarative and imperative sentences end with periods. **Declarative sentences** are those that make statements. Examples:

RIGHT: The mass of men lead lives of quiet desperation.
RIGHT: A foolish consistency is the hobgoblin of little minds.

**Imperative sentences** are those that issue a request or command or give directions. Examples, with the imperative verbs italicized:

RIGHT: *Direct* your eye right inward, and you'll discover a thousand regions in your mind yet undiscovered.
RIGHT: *Travel* them, and *be* expert in home-cosmography.

There are two kinds of **indirect questions:** (1) those which simply state that someone asked something and (2) those that ask for an answer but are not phrased in question form. Periods close each kind. Examples:

RIGHT: The employment agency asked whether I would take a job guarding a gaggle of geese.
RIGHT: I wonder whether you can direct me to Skid Row.

A sentence that includes an indirectly quoted question also ends with a period. An example is: "He asked me if I would like to go swimming." Note that this sort of indirect question must be rephrased from its original form or else enclosed within quotation marks. Example:

WRONG: She asked did I have a few minutes to spare.
RIGHT: She asked if I had a few minutes to spare.
RIGHT: She asked me, "Do you have a few minutes to spare?"

**Courtesy questions** are those in which *will you* is equivalent to *please.* They normally are closed with periods rather than question marks, though a question mark at the end of such a sentence is not wrong. Example:

RIGHT: Will you let me know whether I need to take further action.
RIGHT: Will you let me know whether I need to take further action?

(Periods used with abbreviations are illustrated in Chapter 14.)

# 9B THE QUESTION MARK

### Use a question mark to close a question.

Examples:

RIGHT: Who but the President knows best when national security is at stake?

RIGHT: Has a turn away from open pornography begun yet?

When a question ends a quoted part of a declarative sentence, the question mark goes inside the quotation marks and no additional period is used even though the whole is a statement rather than a question. Example:

RIGHT: The vicar asked, "Have you been playing golf for the past six Sundays?"

When a question in a quoted part of a sentence comes first, a question mark is put inside the quotation marks but no other mark of punctuation separates the quoted part from the remainder. A period closes the whole. Example:

RIGHT: "What is the difference between a metaphor and a symbol?" Luis asked.

A question mark also is used in parentheses to indicate that the immediately preceding information is not certain or is questionable. Example:

RIGHT: The altruism (?) of some tycoons makes them richer.

Information enclosed in parentheses is followed by a question mark when the information is uncertain. Example:

RIGHT: Herodotus (died 428 B.C.?) was the first great historian.

# 9C THE EXCLAMATION POINT

**The exclamation point (or mark) is used to close sentences or nonsentence exclamations or bits of information enclosed in parentheses when the writer wants to show strong emphasis.**

Examples:

RIGHT: We will never, never yield to those insane terrorists!
RIGHT: What irony!
RIGHT: Our first week's sales of *The Reptiles* (25,000 copies!) broke all records for that kind of book.

The exclamation point, however, should be used only sparingly, for the writer who uses the mark very frequently is like the little boy crying "Wolf!" In a short time no reader will believe in the force of any of the exclamation points.

# The Comma

Aside from marks of end punctuation, the comma is by far the most commonly used mark of punctuation and, perhaps because of that, poses more writing problems than any other mark of punctuation. Since rules for punctuation in modern English are almost wholly based on sentence structure, they are mostly precise and fixed. Some options do occur, such as using or not using, according to your pleasure, a comma to separate two short independent clauses joined by a coordinating conjunction. But we will give the basic rules and not elaborate on exceptions, for it is best for you to learn the rules and follow them before you begin to exercise options. Since there are so many rules for the use of the comma, we will use not only our number-letter system of classification but will also number the rules themselves.

In grammar, a constituent is any unified part of a sentence, from single words with specific grammatical functions apart from other words to various kinds of phrases and clauses.

# 10A CONSTITUENTS IN A SERIES

### Rule 1 Use commas to separate three or more constituents in a series.

Examples:

RIGHT: On that scavenger hunt we had to collect a frog, a corset, a bottle with a rye-whisky label, a book printed in French, and a polka-dot bow tie.

RIGHT: When Roscoe will come, what he will do, and when he will leave are questions causing us profound anxiety.

If *two* constituents in a series are not joined by a coordinating conjunction, they should be separated by a comma. Example:

RIGHT: I learned to live without working, to consume without sharing.

# 10B COMPOUND SENTENCES

### Rule 2 Use a comma to separate independent clauses joined by a coordinating conjunction to form one sentence.

The coordinating conjunctions are *and, but, yet, or, nor, for,* and *so.* Examples, with the coordinating conjunctions italicized:

RIGHT: The work proved much harder than the ad had led us to believe, *and* after two hours on the job we walked off without uttering a word.

RIGHT: The Circle K Club ran the prettiest candidate for Homecoming Queen, *yet* she received the fewest votes.

RIGHT: Our group continued working, *for* we feared that the Inquisition would inquire into any idleness on our part.

# 10C  INTRODUCTORY CONSTITUENTS

<u>Rule 3</u>  **Use a comma to set off an introductory constituent whose meaning exhibits some separation from the sentence subject.**

Most sentences open with their subjects, but many open with a word, phrase, or clause that is not a part of the full subject. Such introductory constituents should normally be set off by commas. Examples:

RIGHT: Above, the tree tops were filled with chirping birds.
RIGHT: Unfortunately, our plot to have the final exam canceled did not succeed.
RIGHT: Before leaving, the drugstore manager secretly hired one of the clerks to watch the assistant manager.
RIGHT: Above all, the trees must be sprayed with insecticide.
RIGHT: Please, can we discuss this calmly?
RIGHT: After the disputants both had had their say, the arbitrator retired to reflect on the evidence.
RIGHT: Wearing her wig and carrying an old-fashioned parasol, Madame Gagnon tottered across the lawn toward us.

Introductory adverb clauses and verbal phrases are almost always set off, as in the last two examples, since they are usually followed by a voice pause.

# 10D  TERMINAL CONSTITUENTS

<u>Rule 4</u>  **Use a comma to set off a terminal constituent (one that comes at the end of a sentence) that is preceded by a distinct voice pause.**

Examples:

RIGHT: Ken is just eccentric, not crazy.
RIGHT: The bear looks for ripe berries, and leaves the unripe ones on the bushes.

RIGHT: Many teenagers are not understood by their parents, if by anyone.

(Sometimes terminal constituents are set off by dashes, as is explained in Chapter 11.)

# 10E   PARENTHETIC CONSTITUENTS

<u>Rule 5</u>   **Use commas to set off parenthetic constituents within a sentence.**

A parenthetic constituent is a kind of aside. It is an expression that is not a part of the main sentence but that contains a comment or information that the writer wants to insert within the sentence. Some examples are *as the preacher said, according to my private sources, you will find out, in the first place,* and so on. Also, conjunctive adverbs and transitional phrases that come within an independent clause are considered parenthetic. They are words and phrases such as *however, moreover, for example, in fact,* and so on. Examples:

RIGHT: The highest football score ever, according to the *Guinness Book of Records,* was 222 to 0.

RIGHT: The Tories, you'll soon see, will get us into a depression.

RIGHT: The way to a man's heart, Cheri discovered, is not necessarily through his stomach.

RIGHT: The moral thing to do, nevertheless, is to reveal the whole truth.

RIGHT: The evidence of demonic possession, on the other hand, may be mere misinterpretation of cause and effect.

Of course some introductory and terminal constituents, as shown in Sections 10C and 10D, are by nature parenthetic, but here we are considering only internal parenthetic constituents. Sometimes parenthetic constituents are set off with dashes or parentheses (see Chapter 11).

# 10F ESSENTIAL AND NONESSENTIAL CONSTITUENTS

<u>Rule 6</u>   **Use a comma or commas to set off a nonessential constituent.**

A nonessential constituent, though it may be set off in the same way that a parenthetic constituent is, is not parenthetic but is in the writer's view an essential part of the meaning of the sentence. The grammatical label *nonessential* simply means that if the constituent is removed, the remaining sentence will still be complete and meaningful even though it lacks information the writer wants in it. When an *essential* constituent is removed, the sentence no longer is fully clear and meaningful. Most essential and nonessential constituents are phrases or clauses that modify nouns or are appositives. The key to understanding the difference between them is that an essential constituent is necessary to complete the identification of the noun it is associated with (and thus is not set off with commas) and that a nonessential constituent merely gives additional information about an already-identified noun (and thus requires commas).

The recognition of essential and nonessential constituents poses perhaps the most difficult aspect of English punctuation, and thus further explanations and illustrations are needed. First consider this sentence:

West Point cadets *who break the honor code* are expelled.

The italicized adjective clause is an essential constituent modifying the compound noun *West Point cadets.* It is essential because if it were removed, the noun would not be fully identified, for certainly it is senseless to say *West Point cadets are expelled.* The clause is needed to identify *which* West Point cadets are meant. Thus no commas are called for. Now consider this sentence:

The Commander of West Point, *who personally investigated the cheating scandal,* urged leniency.

The italicized adjective clause modifies *The Commander of West Point,* but that noun phrase carries its own full identification (there is only one Commander of West Point), and thus the adjective clause, which gives additional and not essential information, could be removed and still leave a fully meaningful sentence. The clause, then, is nonessential and is therefore set off with commas.

The ability to punctuate essential and nonessential constituents correctly is especially important because the presence or absence of commas can alter meaning. Two versions of the same sentence, one with commas and one without, can have quite different meanings. For example, consider these sentences:

> The slide rule, which you showed me how to use, has been a help in this course.
>
> The slide rule which you showed me how to use has been a help in this course.

In the first sentence the writer refers to the slide rule as a tool and does not mean any particular slide rule. The clause within commas simply adds nonessential information. In the second sentence the absence of commas shows that the meaning is "this particular slide rule—the one which you showed me how to use." In the millions of sentences you read, it will at times be important for you to interpret punctuation correctly to distinguish such meanings.

Most essential and nonessential constituents are either adjective clauses, adjective phrases, verb phrases, or appositives. Here are further examples, with explanations. The essential or nonessential constituents are italicized.

WRONG: Our Dean of Instruction *who was not appointed President when a vacancy occurred* decided to resign as an administrator.

RIGHT: Our Dean of Instruction, *who was not appointed President when a vacancy occurred,* decided to resign as an administrator.

*Dean of Instruction* is fully identified by *our,* and thus the adjective clause is nonessential and is set off by commas.

As we have noted, some sentences may be correctly punctuated with or without commas around a clause, depending upon the meaning that is intended or is conveyed by the rest of the passage.

RIGHT: The students *who did most of the work building the float* were intensely pro-fraternity.

If the adjective clause is necessary to identify which students are meant, it is essential and thus not set off.

However, if *students* has been fully identified in a previous sentence, its modifier in this sentence is nonessential and thus set off. Example:

RIGHT: We were surrounded by a group of students who were regaling us with odd stories about college homecomings. The students, who did most of the work building the float, were intensely pro-fraternity.

The students are fully identified in the first sentence. This identification carries over into the second sentence so that the adjective clause is nonessential and thus set off. However, this kind of construction is not very common, and therefore we will continue to illustrate with single sentences.

More examples, with adjective phrases italicized:

RIGHT (essential): The wife *happy with her lot in life* is the envy of many of her sisters.
RIGHT (nonessential): Mrs. Wurryfree, *happy with her lot in life,* is puzzled by the high divorce rate.

In the first sentence the phrase is necessary to identify which wife is being discussed. In the second, Mrs. Wurryfree is identified by name and therefore the modifying phrase simply gives additional information.

More examples, with appositives italicized:

WRONG: Raul's wife *Conchita* is president of the local Red Cross chapter.
RIGHT: Raul's wife, *Conchita,* is president of the local Red Cross chapter.

In the wrong sentence, *Conchita* is made essential, thus identifying which of Raul's wives is being mentioned. But since (presumably) Raul has only one wife, *Raul's wife* identifies her, and her name is nonessential information.

WRONG: The German writer, *Hermann Hesse,* is a favorite with college students.

RIGHT: The German writer *Hermann Hesse* is a favorite with college students.

Since Germany has more than one writer, the name is essential to identify which one is under discussion.

RIGHT (if Morley has written only one novel): Richard Morley's novel, *Rotten in Denmark,* has sold only two hundred copies.

RIGHT (if Morley has written more than one novel): Richard Morley's novel *Rotten in Denmark* has sold only two hundred copies.

Further typical examples of incorrectly punctuated sentences from student writing:

WRONG: Emily Dickinson wrote mostly about nature *which she felt had God-like qualities.*

WRONG: I took the case to my counselor *who backed the teacher and gave me no help at all.*

WRONG: We owe many duties to our parents *who nourish and care for us from birth until we can be self-supporting.*

WRONG: We came to the conclusion, *that it takes money to make money.*

*Nature, my counselor,* and *our parents* are fully identified without the italicized adjective clauses; thus the clauses, being nonessential, must be set off with commas. In the last sentence, the clause is essential to identify *conclusion* and thus the comma should *not* precede it.

Nonessential constituents may also be set off with dashes (see Chapter 11).

# 10G  COORDINATE ADJECTIVES

<u>Rule 7</u>  **Use a comma to separate coordinate adjectives which come in front of a noun and are not joined by *and.***

The best definition of coordinate adjectives is that they are two adjectives that would sound natural if joined by *and.* If two modifiers in front of a noun will not sound natural when joined by *and,* they are not coordinate. Examples, with the adjectival modifiers italicized:

SOUNDS UNNATURAL: a *white* and *frame* house
SOUNDS UNNATURAL: a *silly* and *old* man
SOUNDS UNNATURAL: a *purple* and *wool* shawl

Since the adjectives do not sound natural with *and* joining them, they are not coordinate. With the *and* removed they would not be separated by commas. Examples:

RIGHT: a white frame house
RIGHT: a silly old man
RIGHT: a purple wool shawl

Examples of adjectives that do sound natural joined by *and:*

SOUNDS NATURAL: a *well-read* and *intelligent* woman
SOUNDS NATURAL: a *malicious* and *vengeful* old man

These adjectives are coordinate and thus the normal and correct punctuation would be as follows:

RIGHT: a well-read, intelligent woman
RIGHT: a malicious, vengeful old man

Of course more than two coordinate adjectives can occur in front of a noun, in which case all of them would be separated by commas, as in—

RIGHT: a malicious, vengeful, greedy, stubborn, dishonest old man

But in actuality writers do not often use more than two coordinate adjectives in front of a noun.

# 10H ADVERB CLAUSES

**Rule 8   Use a comma or commas to set off an internal or terminal adverb clause when it is separated from the rest of the sentence by a distinct voice pause or pauses.**

Since adverb clauses, which are introduced by subordinating conjunctions, cannot be clearly classified as essential or nonessential (except in the case of *when* and *where* clauses), no rule more definitive than that above can be given for punctuating them. Quite often an internal adverb clause will need to be set off because it requires distinct voice pauses. Examples:

RIGHT: George, since he had a preference for big cars, bought a used Cadillac rather than a new Vega.

RIGHT: The top of the pine tree, after the wind died down, again became a roosting place for a multitude of birds.

A terminal adverb clause may or may not have a voice pause preceding it. In this aspect of punctuation, writers are mostly on their own with no precise rules to guide them. Example:

RIGHT: I refused to pay the repair bill, since my car had been damaged rather than repaired.

But change the *since* to *because* and many professional writers would feel no need for a comma. The subtleties of this aspect of punctuation are too great to be covered in a brief, elementary discussion.

Introductory adverb clauses are normally set off by commas, as rule 3 in Section 10C directs.

# 10I DATES AND ADDRESSES

**Rule 9   In dates use a comma to separate the name of a day from the month and the date of the month from the year.**

Examples:

RIGHT: I predict that an earthquake will occur in San Francisco on Monday, May 5, 1980.

RIGHT: We made a date for Saturday, December 5, 1981, to celebrate our narrow escape from marriage.

When only a month and year are given, no punctuation is necessary. Example:

RIGHT: I can find the proof I want in the June 1974 issue of *Scientific American.*

Some writers like to set off 1974 in such a construction, but the commas serve no useful purpose.

Rule 10   **In addresses use commas to separate the name of a person or establishment from the street address, the street address from the city, and the city from the state.**

Examples:

RIGHT: The fire started at Murphy's Drive-In, 1923 Seventh Street, La Canada, California, and spread throughout a broad area.

RIGHT: At 236 La Cross Avenue, Lureville, New York, is a branch of the infamous Anti-Media Charter Group.

# 10J   MISUSED COMMAS

**Do NOT enter an obstructive comma into any part of a sentence.**

Rule 11   **Do NOT separate a subject from its verb with a single comma.**

Examples:

WRONG: The bill I support, is the one to make all beaches public property.

RIGHT: The bill I support is the one to make all beaches public property.

WRONG: That we were unwelcome, was evident.

RIGHT: That we were unwelcome was evident.

Of course a parenthetic or nonessential constituent set off on both sides may come between a subject and its verb.

Rule 12 **Do NOT separate a verb from its complement (direct object and so on) with a single comma.**

Example:

WRONG: The cause of our breakdown was, that some vandal had put oil in the magneto.
RIGHT: The cause of our breakdown was that some vandal had put oil in the magneto.

Of course a constituent set off on both sides can come between a verb and its complement.

Rule 13 **Do NOT separate noncoordinate adjectives with a comma.**

Examples:

WRONG: Mr. Scearce is an energetic, Baptist preacher.
RIGHT: Mr. Scearce is an energetic Baptist preacher.

WRONG: We saw the suspects in an old, blue Chevrolet.
RIGHT: We saw the suspects in an old blue Chevrolet.

*Energetic and Baptist* and *old and blue* would not sound natural, and thus in each instance the two modifiers are not coordinate.

Rule 14 **Do NOT separate two constituents in a series joined by a coordinating conjunction.**

Example:

WRONG: My only obligation is to follow my conscience, and to help the unfortunate.
RIGHT: My only obligation is to follow my conscience and to help the unfortunate.

# The Dash; Parentheses; Brackets; the Colon

## 11A USES OF THE DASH

As a mark of punctuation, the dash has uses similar to some uses of the comma. Generally it is used when, for emphasis, the writer wants a pause slightly longer than a comma calls for or when other commas in the sentence make dashes necessary for clarity. On the typewriter a dash is made with two hyphens (--). In a sentence no space is left before or after a dash.

**Rule 1** **Use dashes to set off a parenthetic comment that is very long or that is a complete sentence itself.**

Examples:

RIGHT: You may say many wise things▬you who have lived past your allotted three score years and ten▬, but we young will continue to listen to our own inner voices.

RIGHT: I wrote these words▬I was completely isolated at the time▬when my pessimism had reached its greatest depth.

In the first example, the comma after the second dash is also correct, for it would be needed if the whole parenthetic constituent were removed (see 10B). Parentheses instead of dashes would be wrong because the writers want the inter-polated comments to stand out boldly rather than having something of the nature of a footnote. Commas instead of dashes would be correct in the first example but would not provide the emphasis that the dashes do.

Rule 2 **Use a dash or dashes to set off a nonessential constituent that is especially emphatic or that contains commas of its own.**

Examples:

RIGHT: The nation's most popular sport━bowling!━now attracts more than thirty percent of the population.

RIGHT: Our leader's coded message━written in blood━had us all wild with curiosity.

In these cases the writers wanted to add emphasis to their nonessential constituents and thus used dashes instead of commas to set them off.

RIGHT: All of the humanities━literature, philosophy, drama, art history, rhetoric, and the fine arts━are experiencing in-creasing enrollments.

Since the nonessential appositive has commas of its own, commas to set it off would cause confusion. Dashes provide clarity.

Rule 3 **Use a dash to give emphasis to a constituent that would not normally be set off at all.**

Example:

RIGHT: Those corrupt politicians deserve credit for giving Ameri-cans an overdue━and much-needed━civics lesson.

*And much-needed* need not be set off at all, but the writer set it off with dashes in order to emphasize it. Commas would provide some emphasis but not as much as dashes.

**Rule 4    Use a dash to set off a terminal constituent that is an explanation of a preceding constituent or that is a very distinct afterthought.**

Examples:

RIGHT: Strawn resorted to his only hope—plea bargaining.
RIGHT: The best way to settle an argument is to speak softly—or buy drinks all around.

In the first example, a colon after *hope* would also be correct but more formal. In the second example, only a dash will produce the delayed-afterthought effect the writer wanted.

**Rule 5    Use a dash to set off an initial series of constituents which is then summarized by a noun or pronoun that serves as the sentence subject.**

Examples:

RIGHT: Federalists, Whigs, Know-Nothings, Dixiecrats, Bull Moosers, Progressives—all are vanished political labels.
RIGHT: Tax reform, environmental clean-up, more federal aid to education, revision of welfare laws, reduction in armaments, lower unemployment—these changes were the candidate's stated goals.

The pronouns *all* and *these* are used to summarize the initial constituents in order to emphasize them.

**Caution:** Do *not* use dashes instead of periods as end punctuation.

# 11B  USES OF PARENTHESES

The word *parentheses* is plural, meaning both the curved marks that go by that name (*parenthesis* is the singular). A space is used outside a parenthesis unless another mark of punctuation follows it, but no space is used on the inside of a parenthesis. If an entire sentence following a mark of end punctuation is enclosed in parentheses, the period to close the sentence goes inside the final parenthesis. If only the terminal part of a sentence is enclosed in parentheses, the period closing the sentence goes outside the parenthesis. If a complete sentence enclosed in parentheses does not come after a mark of end punctuation, the period closing the entire sentence goes outside the parenthesis.

<u>Rule 6</u>  **Use parentheses to enclose any kind of parenthetic or nonessential constituent — even a sentence or group of sentences — when such a constituent has a tone of isolation from the main sentence and is intended to be an aside.**

Examples:

RIGHT: We continued to frolic with carefree abandon (later we would learn that we had troubles).

The writer does not intend to discuss the troubles at this point; hence the parenthetic comment is in parentheses, which isolate it more than a dash would. Note that even though the enclosed construction is a complete sentence, the period closing the whole sentence goes outside the parenthesis because the nonenclosed sentence does not have end punctuation. Another correct way of punctuating this construction is this:

RIGHT: We continued to frolic with careless abandon. (Later we would learn that we had troubles.)

RIGHT: In 1933 Norris Baxter (later to become a movie star) attracted much attention with his theory of orgones.

Parentheses rather than dashes or commas set off this constituent because it has a tone of isolation, or something of the nature of a footnote.

RIGHT: Both Turner and Avinger were refusing to sign contracts. (Grady and Towle had signed as early as February, but they were hardly star players. Tooey had signed, too, but he alone could not constitute a pitching staff.) Not only were they asking for huge salary increases but also for other concessions. . . .

The enclosed two sentences are an aside, not directly a part of the discussion of Turner and Avinger. Note that the *they* of the last sentence refers to Turner and Avinger, not to the names within the parentheses. Also note that the period goes inside the parentheses because complete sentences are enclosed.

Rule 7  **Use parentheses to enclose numerals used to number items in a series.**

Example:

RIGHT: The five most useful spelling rules are (1) the doubling-of-the-final-consonant rule, (2) the dropping-of-the-silent e rule, (3) the retention-of-the-silent e rule, (4) the y-to-i rule, and (5) the ie-ei rule.

Note that the conjunction *and* precedes the parentheses that enclose the last item.

Rule 8  **Use parentheses to enclose cross-references and bits of information inserted so as not to be a part of the grammatical structure of the sentence.**

Example:

RIGHT: Deism (see also Natural Religion) was most vigorously promoted by Thomas Paine (1737–1809).

The first enclosure is a cross-reference. The second enclosure is information — birth and death dates — that the writer wanted to insert without composing another sentence or large constituent in order to do so.

# 11C  USES OF BRACKETS

Square brackets [like the ones enclosing this phrase] should not be confused with parentheses.

Rule 9  **Use brackets to enclose nonquoted material inserted into a direct quotation for the purpose of clarification.**

Example:

RIGHT: "She [Maria Wilson] was found guilty as an accomplice in the murder and received a fifteen-year sentence."

The writer wished to use a direct quotation, but the readers would not have known the reference of the pronoun *she.* Therefore the reference is given in brackets for clarification.

Rule 10  **Use brackets to enclose comments inserted into direct quotations.**

Such insertions may be information included to make a quotation intelligible or personal comments. Examples:

RIGHT: "I got into English 50 because my consalar [sic] advised me to take it."

The word *sic* means *thus* and is used by the writer to indicate that the error was in the original quotation.

RIGHT: "I have endeavored to cooperate in every way possible [a gross overstatement] with the committee."

Here the writer wanted to insert a personal comment at the appropriate place rather than to delay the comment until the quotation was ended.

# 11D  USES OF THE COLON

The colon is a mark of punctuation used to introduce various kinds of constituents or longer passages of discourse.

Rule 11  **Use a colon after the salutation in a formal letter.**

Examples:

FORMAL: Dear Professor Burnsides:
INFORMAL: Dear Millie,

Rule 12  **Use a colon after an introductory label.**

Examples:

INCORRECT:  Peel them potatoes.
CORRECT:  Peel those potatoes.

<u>Rule 13</u>   **Use a colon to introduce a series which is prepared for in the main clause of a sentence.**

Example:

RIGHT: My deductions were as follows**:** the student has a photographic memory; she had read the chapter carefully; in her term paper she unconsciously used the wording of the original as though it were her own.

<u>Rule 14</u>   **A colon may be used after a sentence that introduces a direct quotation.**

Example:

RIGHT: It was William James who said**:** "To *know* is one thing, and to know for certain *that* we know is another. One may hold to the first being possible without the second."

<u>Rule 15</u>   **A colon may be used to introduce a terminal constituent that is an explanation.**

Example:

RIGHT: I was left with but one desire**:** an hour of solitude.

A dash after *desire* would also be correct, though more informal.

<u>Rule 16</u>   **Do NOT use a colon directly after the verbs *are* and *were*.**

Instead, use no punctuation at all, or use such a word as *these* or *the following* after *are* or *were* and before the colon. Examples:

POOR STYLE: The facts in the case were: the defendant had not been advised of his rights; the arresting officer has used unnecessary force; and the crime violated a law that had not been invoked for over fifty years.

PROPER STYLE: The facts in the case were the following**:** the defendant had not been advised of his rights; the arresting officer had used unnecessary force; and the crime violated a law that had not been invoked for over fifty years.

WRONG: The most distant planets are: Uranus, Neptune, and Pluto.
RIGHT:   The most distant planets are Uranus, Neptune, and Pluto.

# The Semicolon

A general rule is that semicolons are used to separate only coordinate, not noncoordinate, constituents. The semicolon calls for a voice pause as long as that of a period, but it is used only as internal punctuation.

## 12 A COMPOUND SENTENCES WITHOUT CONNECTIVES

Rule 1 **Use a semicolon to separate two independent clauses that form a compound sentence but that do not have a connective word between them.**

Examples:

RIGHT: My losses mounted steadily; I began to fear that my roulette system had a flaw of some sort.

RIGHT: The jet was hardly above tree-top level; its deafening scream added to the fright of the neighborhood's residents.

Writers use such compound sentences because they do not want to separate such closely related clauses into separate sentences. Note particularly that semicolons are required between the clauses; commas would produce comma splices (see Chapter 3).

# 12B COMPOUND SENTENCES WITH CONNECTIVES

<u>Rule 2</u>  **Use a semicolon to separate two independent clauses joined by a connective other than a coordinating conjunction.**

When independent clauses are joined by a coordinating conjunction, they usually need only a comma between them. When they are connected by a conjunctive adverb or a transitional phrase, they must be separated by a semicolon unless they are punctuated as separate sentences. Sometimes the conjunctive adverb or transitional phrase is shifted to the interior of the second clause. Examples:

RIGHT: The Purple Frogs failed to show up for their scheduled rock concert; however, a local group, the Flat Tires, substituted.
RIGHT: Our college always offers a course for far-out students; for example, last semester the Biology Department offered a course in exobiology, the study of life on other planets.
RIGHT: We learned that the rapids were very swift; several of us, however, got into the boats.

The semicolons in these examples are necessary, unless each example were punctuated as two sentences. Commas in place of the semicolons would produce comma splices (see Chapter 3).

# 12C CONSTITUENTS IN A SERIES

<u>Rule 3</u>  **Use semicolons to separate constituents in a series when the constituents have internal punctuation of their own or when they are especially long.**

Examples:

RIGHT: We were directed to separate the debris into three piles: (1) cans, bottles, and plastic containers; (2) scrap metal, rubber, and sheet plastic; and (3) stucco, bricks, mortar, and concrete.

Since each of the three parts of the series has commas of its own, semicolons clarify the structure. Note that the semicolons still separate coordinate constituents. Also note that this example illustrates one use of the colon and one use of parentheses.

RIGHT: Professor Means's study showed that American Indians from reservations made lower average scores on standardized tests than Indians living off reservations; that Indians who live in a stable community scored higher than those who are migrant; and that Indians tested in their own languages scored higher on I.Q. tests than Indians tested in English.

Because the constituents in a series in this example are so long, the semicolons make the sentence structure clearer than commas would, though commas would be acceptable.

# 12D MISUSED SEMICOLONS

### Rule 4   Do NOT use a semicolon between noncoordinate constituents.

Example:

WRONG: Because of the heavy freeze, our water pipes had burst; the main valve not having been shut off the night before.

RIGHT:  Because of the heavy freeze, our water pipes had burst, the main valve . . .

A comma should replace the semicolon since the second constituent is not an independent clause and thus is not coordinate with the constituent that precedes the semicolon.

<u>Rule 5</u>   **Do NOT use a semicolon after the connective** *such as.*

Example:

WRONG: We chose several kinds of books, such as; fiction, travel
books, psychology texts, and *Playboy* joke books.
RIGHT:   We chose several kinds of books, such as fiction, travel
books . . .

<u>Rule 6</u>   **Do NOT use a semicolon in place of a dash or colon.**

Examples:

WRONG: Just one thing kept me from carrying out my plan; lack of
money.
RIGHT:   Just one thing kept me from carrying out my plan—lack
of money.

WRONG: On this particular job I had four duties; to open the store
in the morning and prepare for customers, to restock the
shelves, to carry empty boxes and such to the outside
trash bins, and occasionally to wait on customers when
everybody else was busy.
RIGHT:   On this particular job I had four duties: to open the
store . . .

# Quotation Marks

## 13A DIRECT QUOTATIONS

Rule 1    **Enclose direct quotations in quotation marks.**

Examples:

RIGHT: Feuer maintained that "a minority of students are turning to shallow faculties on the outskirts of the universities where a variety of [charlatans] . . . offer courses in which they provide answers as well as questions."

This is the kind of direct quotation that might appear in a term paper. (Note that square brackets enclose material not in the direct quotation but entered by the writer for clarification. Also note that three spaced periods indicate ellipsis, or omission of part of the quotation.)

RIGHT: He maintained that children are "credulous" and "unresistant to indoctrination."

When such a connective as *and* joins two quoted units, as in the above example, each quoted unit is enclosed in quotation marks but the unquoted connective word is not.

RIGHT: Rodney asked, "Will you join the organization?"
"No."
"Then you must not repeat anything you have heard tonight."

This is an example of direct quotations as they are used in dialogue in fiction.

## 13B   QUOTATIONS WITHIN QUOTATIONS

<u>Rule 2</u>   **When a direct quotation is used within a direct quotation, enclose the internal quotation in single quotation marks and the whole quotation in regular quotation marks.**

Example:

RIGHT: The commencement speaker said: "In Ecclesiastes we read that 'In much wisdom is much grief, and he who increaseth knowledge increaseth sorrow,' but we must still pursue knowledge for the fulfillment of God's will."

Also the constituents covered in rules 3, 4, 5, and 6 in Sections 13C and 13D should be enclosed in single quotation marks if they appear within a direct quotation.

## 13C   TITLES

<u>Rule 3</u>   **Use quotation marks to enclose the quoted titles of short stories, short poems, one-act plays, essays, chapters, and other literary works of less than book or three-act-play length.**

Examples:

RIGHT: E. A. Robinson's poem "Mr. Flood's Party" is about an old man who has outlived his time.

RIGHT: **"**The Capital of the World**"** is one of Hemingway's best
    stories.

RIGHT: The third chapter of *The Scarlet Letter* is entitled **"**The
    Recognition.**"**

RIGHT: Professor Lucy Phurr distinctly said, **"**Read Melville's short
    story **'**Bartleby the Scrivener**'** by tomorrow.**"**

Note the single quotation marks enclosing the title in the
last example.

    Titles of book-length literary works are underlined in
longhand and italicized in print (see Section 14B). No title
should ever be both underlined and enclosed in quotation
marks.

**Rule 4** **Do NOT put quotation marks around a title used
as the heading of a theme or essay.**

Of course if a quoted unit is included in the title, that unit is
enclosed in quotation marks. Examples:

TITLE AS HEADING: How Nellie Paid the Mortgage on the Farm

TITLE AS HEADING: A Study of Christian Symbols in Steinbeck's
    **"**The Flight**"**

If the second title appeared in a paragraph, the whole title
would be in regular quotation marks and the title of the
story in single quotation marks.

# 13D   SPECIAL CONSTITUENTS

**Rule 5** **A word used as a word and not for its meaning
may be enclosed in quotation marks.**

Examples:

RIGHT: Both **"**tomato**"** and **"**tart**"** are commonly used as slang
    terms.

RIGHT: Ling Chan's proposal contained too many **"**if's.**"**

Also, words used as words may be underlined in longhand
and italicized in print (see Section 14B), but never are they
both underlined and put in quotation marks.

<u>Rule 6</u>  **Use quotation marks to enclose a word or phrase used in a special or ironical sense.**

Examples:

RIGHT: Mona feels that she must belong to the "right set."
RIGHT: The "justice" of the verdict was enough to make me cry.

In the first example, the quotation marks mean that the writer's concept of what is the right set is different from Mona's—that is, that Mona only thinks that the set she belongs to is special or worthy of praise. In the second example, the quotation marks mean that the writer did not think the verdict represented justice at all.

You should avoid enclosing slang terms in quotation marks as an apology for their use. Example:

POOR USAGE: Claudette has a "hang-up" about rich boys trying to date her.
BETTER: Claudette has a hang-up about rich boys trying to date her.

If a slang term is wortn using, use it without apology.

# 13E WITH OTHER MARKS OF PUNCTUATION

<u>Rule 7</u>  **Always put periods and commas inside rather than outside quotation marks, regardless of whether the period or comma belongs to the quoted unit.**

Examples:

RIGHT: I decided to entitle my paper "Existentialism in *Moby-Dick*."
RIGHT: Although our preacher says "The way of the transgressor is hard," I notice that our local crooks have an easy time of it.

Neither the period in the first example nor the comma in the second belongs to the quoted unit, but each is correctly placed within the quotation marks.

<u>Rule 8</u>   **Marks of punctuation other than the period and the comma are placed inside quotation marks when they are a part of the quoted unit and outside the quotation marks when they are not a part of the quoted unit.**

Examples:

RIGHT: Did Professor Gallegos say "to chapter ten" or "through chapter ten"?

Since the question mark does not belong to the quoted unit, it is placed outside the quotation marks.

RIGHT: Ann Landers was heard to utter, "Why am I so lonely?"

Since the question mark belongs to the quoted unit, it is placed inside the quotation marks. Note also that no additional period is used even though the whole sentence is a statement and not a question.

RIGHT: Franklin said, "He who hesitates is lost"; he also said, "Look before you leap."

The semicolon is not a part of the quoted unit and thus is placed outside the quotation marks.

# Mechanics

## 14A MANUSCRIPT FORM

### 14A1 For Handwritten Papers

Observe the following directions in preparing handwritten papers:

1. Use blue or black ink, if possible. Never use red or reddish ink.
2. Write on lined 8½ x 11 notebook paper.
3. Do not skip every other line unless the notepaper is narrow-spaced. Avoid narrow-spaced paper, if possible.
4. Write on one side of the paper only.
5. Compose a title (not just a statement of the topic) for your paper. Skip a line between the title and the first line of your paper.

6. Do *not* enclose your title in quotation marks and do *not* underline it. A unit within the title, such as the title of a short story or a word used in a special sense (see Section 13D), should be enclosed in quotation marks. The title of a book within your paper's title should be underlined.

7. Do not write outside the left-hand margin line (usually in red, if there is one), except to put numbers of questions if you are writing a test.

8. Leave at least a half-inch margin on the right-hand side of your notebook paper; do not crowd the right-hand side nor write down the right-hand margin. Also do not leave an excessively wide right-hand margin.

9. Use a hyphen to divide a word at the end of a line and divide *only* between syllables. Do *not* divide a one-syllable word, such as *twel-ve* or *walk-ed.* Do *not* divide a word so that a single letter is set apart, such as *a-bove* or *pun-y.* Consult a dictionary, if necessary, for syllabication.

10. Never let a mark of end punctuation, a comma, a semi-colon, or a colon begin a line of your paper. Never end a line with the first of a set of quotation marks, parentheses, or brackets.

11. Indent each paragraph about one inch.

12. Make corrections neatly. Do not leave errors enclosed in parentheses. Try to make every physical aspect of your paper neat. Proofread carefully.

13. Follow your instructor's directions for folding your paper and entering your name and other information on it.

## 14A2   For Typewritten Papers

Observe the following directions in preparing typewritten papers:

1. Use unruled 8½ x 11 bond paper, if possible. Do not use onionskin paper.

2. Avoid using a red-ink ribbon. Type on one side of the paper only.
3. For your title, follow directions 5 and 6 in Section 14A1.
4. Double space between the lines of your paper (except for inset quotations and footnotes in a term paper).
5. Double space horizontally (that is, use two typewriter spaces instead of one) after all marks of end punctuation and colons.
6. Single space after commas, semicolons, parentheses, and brackets.
7. Make a dash with two hyphens (--) and leave no space before or after a dash.
8. When underlining to show italics, underline the spaces between words too, unless your instructor gives you different instructions.
9. To make the numeral 1, use the small letter l on the keyboard, *not* the capital i.
10. Use Arabic numerals (1, 2, 3, 4, and so on) rather than Roman numerals (I, II, III, IV, and so on) to number pages.
11. Follow direction 9 in Section 14A1 for dividing words at the end of a line.
12. Maintain a 1¼-inch margin on the left-hand side of each page and about a one-inch margin on the other three sides. Of course the right-hand ends of lines in typewriting, as in longhand, will be uneven.
13. Indent paragraphs five spaces.
14. Keep your paper neat and proofread it carefully.
15. Follow your instructor's directions for folding your paper and entering your name and other information on it.

# 14B  UNDERLINING AND QUOTATION MARKS

Underlining in longhand or typing is equivalent to italics in print. Underlining and quotation marks are linked in certain ways.

## 14B1   Underlining

<u>Rule 1</u>   **Underline titles of book-length literary works, newspapers, magazines, musical compositions, works of art, and names of ships and aircraft.**

Examples:

RIGHT: Mark Twain's <u>Tom Sawyer</u>
Shakespeare's <u>Romeo and Juliet</u>
Milton's <u>Paradise Lost</u>
<u>Harper's</u> magazine (Only the name of the magazine is under-lined.)
the Los Angeles <u>Times</u> (The city is not usually underlined.)
Handel's <u>The Messiah</u> (a musical composition)
Degas' <u>The Dancer and the Bouquet</u> (a painting)
the <u>Titanic</u> (a ship)
<u>Air Force One</u> (an individual aircraft)

<u>Rule 2</u>   **Underline foreign words and phrases that have not been fully Anglicized.**

Consult a dictionary if necessary. Examples:

RIGHT: The <u>sine qua non</u> of science is accuracy.
RIGHT: The <u>raison d'être</u> of freshman composition is employment for English teachers.

<u>Rule 3</u>   **Words or phrases used as words or phrases and not for their meaning may be underlined.**

Examples:

RIGHT: The slang phrase <u>out of sight</u> originated in the nineteenth century.
RIGHT: Professor Stone's inaccurate use of <u>epistemology</u> confused his students.

Words used as words may be enclosed in quotation marks, but they are never both underlined and enclosed in quotation marks.

<u>Rule 4</u>   **Words or phrases may be underlined for emphasis.**

Examples:

RIGHT: I kept quiet precisely because I <u>didn't</u> want the defendant found not guilty.

RIGHT: For human survival we must discontinue <u>all arms manufac-turing</u>.

Single words or short phrases, such as *not,* may be capital-ized, instead of underlined, for emphasis. However, under-lining or capitalization for emphasis should be used judi-ciously, for overuse will cause readers to lose faith in the need for emphasis.

## 14B2  Quotation Marks

The use of quotation marks for enclosing direct quotations is covered in Chapter 13. Here we discuss these marks only as they are related to underlining (italics). Periods and commas are always put inside quotation marks, even when they are not a part of the quoted unit. Other marks of punc-tuation are put inside quotation marks when they are part of the quoted unit and outside when they are not part of the quoted unit. See Section 13E for examples.

<u>Rule 5</u>  **Use quotation marks to enclose titles of short stories, short poems, one-act plays, essays, chapters, and other literary works of less than book or three-act-play length.**

Examples:

RIGHT: Frost's poem "Birches"
Faulkner's short story "That Evening Sun"
Fred Jacobs's short play "Golden Land"
Thoreau's essay "Civil Disobedience"
Chapter 14 is entitled "The Campaign of '48."

No title is ever both underlined and enclosed in quotation marks.

<u>Rule 6</u>   **Do not put a title used as a heading in quotation marks.**

Units within the title as heading may, however, be enclosed in quotation marks. Examples:

TITLE AS HEADING: Abroad with Two Yanks
TITLE AS HEADING: The History of "Gab" as Slang

<u>Rule 7</u>   **A word or phrase used as a word or phrase and not for its meaning may be enclosed in quotation marks.**

Examples:

RIGHT: "Biddable" is one of the most euphonious words in English.
RIGHT: The expression "rattle your cage" is a merging of two slang terms.

Also, words used as words may be underlined, but never both underlined and enclosed in quotation marks.

<u>Rule 8</u>   **Use quotation marks to enclose a word or phrase used in a special ironic sense.**

Example:

RIGHT: Bernie likes to think he is a member of the "literary" set.

The quotation marks mean that the writer does not think Bernie's set has real literary attributes.

# 14C   ABBREVIATIONS

Rules for using abbreviations vary considerably, as you will observe in your reading. The rules given here are an acceptable guide for the sort of writing done in English composition courses. They do not apply to such writing as addresses on envelopes, lists, technical data, and other special forms of composition.

## 14C1    Abbreviations Acceptable in All Kinds of Writing

**Rule 9    Use the following abbreviations designating individuals:**

| | |
|---|---|
| Mr. | Mmes. (plural of Mrs.) |
| Mrs. | St. (Saint) |
| Ms. (any female) | Sr. |
| Messrs. (plural of Mr.) | Jr. |

**Rule 10    Use abbreviations to designate any earned or honorary degree or special awards.**

Examples:

DEGREES: A.B.
B.A.
M.A.
M.D. (medical doctor)
Ph.D. (doctor of philosophy)
Ed.D. (doctor of education)
D.D.S. (doctor of dental science)
D.D. (doctor of divinity)
J.D. (doctor of jurisprudence)
D.V.M. (doctor of veterinary medicine)
D.Lit. *or* D.Litt. (doctor of literature)
LL.D. (doctor of laws)
D.H.L. (doctor of Hebrew literature)

SPECIAL AWARDS: O.M. (Order of Merit: English)
D.S.C. (Distinguished Service Cross)
D.S.M. (Distinguished Service Medal)

**Rule 11    Use the following abbreviations designating time:**

1800 B.C. (before Christ)
A.D. 1462 (in the year of our Lord)
DST, PST (daylight saving time, Pacific standard time, and so on)
4:12 A.M. *or* 4:12 a.m.
3:30 P.M. *or* 3:30 p.m.

<u>Rule 12</u>  **Use abbreviations to designate well-known agencies, organizations, and unions, either governmental or private.**

Examples:

| | |
|---|---|
| UN | CIA |
| UNESCO | VA |
| WHO | VFW |
| CARE | ILGWU |
| CAB | UAW |

While such abbreviations usually appear with no periods, you may use periods if you wish. The important thing is to be consistent and to make sure your usage will be clear to the reader.

<u>Rule 13</u>  **Frequently-used technical terms may be abbreviated.**

Examples:

| | |
|---|---|
| mpg (miles per gallon) | rpm (revolutions per minute) |
| mph (miles per hour) | BTU (British thermal unit) |

<u>Rule 14</u>  **The abbreviations *no., nos.,* and $ are acceptable when used with numerals.**

Examples:

RIGHT: The winner was no. 4238.
RIGHT: Please pay particular attention to nos. 2, 6, 9, and 13.
RIGHT: My plumbing bill was $1239.62.

<u>Rule 15</u>  **The following abbreviations of standard foreign phrases may be used.** They normally are italicized.

| | |
|---|---|
| *i.e.* (that is) | *viz.* (namely) |
| *e.g.* (for example) | *cf.* (compare with) |
| *c.* (*circa:* about) | |

<u>Rule 16</u>  **In purely technical writing abbreviations of technical terms are acceptable.**

Examples:

| | |
|---|---|
| cc. (cubic centimeter) | gm. (gram) |
| cm. (centimeter) | in. (inch) |

The examples in the above eight rules are representative. Other abbreviations of the same sort are acceptable. When in doubt, consult a dictionary.

## 14C2  Abbreviations to Be Avoided in Semiformal Writing

<u>Rule 17</u>   **Avoid abbreviating titles of individuals** (except as specified in Section 14C1, Rule 9).

Examples:

WRONG: The *Pres.* will hold a press conference today.
RIGHT:   The **President** will hold a press conference today.

WRONG: The committee includes *Prof.* Dingbat and *Sen.* Jonas.
RIGHT:   The committee includes **Professor** Dingbat and **Senator** Jonas.

<u>Rule 18</u>   **Avoid abbreviating first names.**

Examples:

WRONG: Benj.        Geo.        Jas.        Theo.

<u>Rule 19</u>   **Avoid abbreviating the names of states, provinces, and countries.**

Examples:

WRONG: The Holdens went to *N. Y.* for their vacation.
RIGHT:   The Holdens went to **New York** for their vacation.

WRONG: Professor Ainsley spent her sabbatical in *Eng.*
RIGHT:   Professor Ainsley spent her sabbatical in **England.**

<u>Rule 20</u>   **Avoid abbreviating the names of days, months, and seasons.**

Examples:

WRONG: The last day of *Feb.* falls on a *Thurs.* this year.
RIGHT:　The last day of **February** falls on a **Thursday** this year.

Rule 21　**Avoid abbreviating names of streets, avenues, boulevards, and courts.**

Examples:

WRONG: Phil just bought a house on Baylor *St.*
RIGHT:　Phil just bought a house on Baylor **Street.**

Rule 22　**Avoid abbreviating the word *company* and avoid the ampersand (&), unless it is part of the name of a firm.**

Examples:

WRONG: the Johnsons & the Smollets
RIGHT:　the Johnsons **and** the Smollets

WRONG: T. L. Floyd *& Co.* is an equal-opportunity employer.
RIGHT:　T. L. Floyd **& Company** is an equal-opportunity employer.

Rule 23　**Avoid the abbreviation Xmas.**

Rule 24　**Avoid abbreviating weights and measurements.**

Examples:

| WRONG: | | RIGHT: | |
|--------|--------|--------|--------|
| oz. | | ounces | |
| lbs. | | pounds | |
| ft. | | foot *or* feet | |
| yds. | | yards | |

Rule 25　**Avoid abbreviating common words.**

Examples:

| WRONG: | | RIGHT: | |
|--------|--------|--------|--------|
| yrs. | | years *or* yours | |
| bldg. | | building | |
| sch. | | school | |
| Rom. C. | | Roman Catholic | |
| con't. | | continued | |
| gov't. | | government | |

# 14D   NUMERALS

Although usage varies, the following rules for the use of numerals and spelled-out numbers are a satisfactory guide.

<u>Rule 26</u>   **For random figures, spell out numbers that require no more than two words; use numerals for numbers that would require more than two words if spelled out.**

Examples:

PREFERRED: There are **five thousand** students in our college, but only **thirty-three** are taking calculus.

PREFERRED: The *Times* estimated that **three million** voters would go to the polls; the exact figure was **3,002,473.**

PREFERRED: This year we had **174** school days.

In the second example, note the use of commas without spaces in the large figure written in numerals.

<u>Rule 27</u>   **In a sentence or passage that contains a series of figures, use numerals for all of them.**

Example:

PREFERRED: My unit sales for each of my first seven work days were **9, 22, 8, 101, 61, 3,** and **102.**

Note that the word *seven* is written out, since it is not part of the series.

<u>Rule 28</u>   **Use numerals in dates, addresses, and time when accompanied by A.M. or P.M.**

Examples:

RIGHT: July **11, 1922** *or* (military and technical style) **11** July **1922.**

RIGHT: **242** Columbus Street, Apartment **3B**

RIGHT: Room **701,** Hotel Padre

RIGHT: **8:22** A.M.

On checks and other such writing, dates may be written in this way: 7-11-22 *or* 7/11/22.

Rule 29  **Use numerals to state measurements, page numbers, and money used with $.**

Examples:

RIGHT: Professor Mole's research notes are all on **4″ x 6″** index cards.
RIGHT: That high school basketball center is **6′ 11″** tall.
RIGHT: The information is on pages **3** and **26** of the *World Almanac*.
RIGHT: Our surplus was **$26.13.**

But when simple, nonfractional numbers are involved, they may be spelled out. Examples:

RIGHT: Our rival's center is nearly **seven** feet tall.
RIGHT: We expect **twenty dollars** to be sufficient.

Rule 30  **When decimals or fractions are involved, use numerals.**

Examples:

RIGHT: My average weight loss was **2.65** pounds per day for a week.
RIGHT: No longer can one borrow money at **5 3/4** percent interest.

Rule 31  **Use numerals for code numbers, such as Social Security numbers, air flight numbers, and telephone numbers.**

Examples:

RIGHT: My Army serial number was **34571285.**
RIGHT: You may reach me by phone at **871-7120,** extension **242.**
RIGHT: United's Flight **23** was delayed an hour.

Rule 32  **To prevent misreading when two numbers appear consecutively, spell out the first one and use numerals for the other.**

Example:

RIGHT: I caught **six 8-inch** trout.

Rule 33  **Except in purely technical writing, do not open a sentence with numerals.**

Examples:

POOR STYLE: *1250* partisan voters attended the rally.
PREFERRED: **Twelve hundred and fifty** partisan voters attended the rally.

<u>Rule 34</u>   **Except in legal and commercial writing, it is not good style to enter numerals in parentheses after a spelled-out number.**

Example:

INAPPROPRIATE STYLE: I purchased *twenty-five (25)* paperback books at the College Bookstore's recent sale.
BETTER: I purchased **twenty-five** paperback books . . .

# 14E   CONTRACTIONS

Nowadays, contractions such as *won't, doesn't, shouldn't,* and so on appear in semiformal writing in such magazines as *Harper's, Consumer Reports, Science News,* and so on and in many books of nonfiction. Opinion among English teachers, however, is divided as to whether contractions should be allowed in writing assigned in college composition courses. You should ascertain your instructor's preference and follow it.

# SECTION THREE

# SPELLING

# Spelling Rules

English spelling is, as everyone knows, full of irregularities which make spelling a difficult subject. But there is much regularity in our spelling system, too, and the irregularities are for the most part rather narrowly limited. For example, the sound /f/ is not always spelled *f,* but it is always spelled either *f* (as in *fit*), *ff* (as in *buff*), *ph* (as in *photo*), or *gh* (as in *laugh*) and so has a degree of regularity. Thus, though English spelling is hard and most people have trouble with it, an understanding of its regularities can improve anyone's spelling. There are several spelling rules that are highly useful to everyone who masters them, for they give much insight into the regularities of English spelling. (There are spelling rules other than those that follow, but they are so riddled with exceptions and so hard to remember that they are not very useful.)

x

# 15A THE DOUBLING-OF-THE-FINAL-CONSONANT RULE

The doubling-of-the-final-consonant rule is complex but applies to a great many common words. The rule:

Rule 1 **When adding a suffix beginning with a vowel to a word which is accented on the last syllable and which ends in a single consonant preceded by a single vowel, double the final consonant.**

The accented or stressed syllable is the one spoken with most force. For example, we accent the last syllable of *re-FER,* but we accent the first syllable of *SUF-fer.*

This complicated rule is based on an important phonetic principle in English spelling called the long-vowel, short-vowel principle, which has two parts. First, in a vowel-consonant-vowel sequence the first vowel, *if it is in an accented syllable,* is long. Thus in *debate* the a-t-e sequence in the accented syllable causes the *a* to be long. Second, in a vowel-final consonant sequence or a vowel-consonant-consonant sequence, the vowel is short. Thus in *bat* the a-t sequence at the end makes the *a* short; also in *batted* the a-t-t sequence keeps the *a* short. There are, inevitably in English, many exceptions to this principle, but it is regular enough to be highly useful, both in understanding the doubling-of-the-final-consonant rule (which is almost always regular) and in understanding many other words. For example a great many people misspell *occasion* by using two *s*'s instead of one, which misspelling would give the pronunciation *o-KASS-yun* instead of the correct *o-KAY-zyun.* Understanding the long-vowel, short-vowel principle prevents such mistakes.

Here are some more examples of the principle at work:

| long vowels | short vowels |
|---|---|
| rate | rat |
| Pete | pet |
| bite | bit |
| rote | rot |
| cure | cur |

In the first column the silent *e*'s — forming a vowel-consonant-vowel sequence — make the first vowel long. In the
second column the vowels are short because the second
consonant ends the word. The whole purpose of the
doubling-of-the-final-consonant rule is to preserve the
short vowel sound in such words as *dis-BAR*, *re-FER*, *ad-
MIT* and *dot* when a suffix beginning with a vowel is added
to them. (The letters *a* and *e* have more than one short-vowel
sound so far as this rule is concerned.)

Since the rule is complex, here again are the three main
parts of it:

1. The suffix added must begin with a vowel. Such suffixes
   are *ing, ed, er, est, able, y,* and so on.
2. The word to which the suffix is added must be accented
   on the last syllable. All one-syllable words and such
   words as *pre-FER*, *oc-CUR*, and *com-PEL* are examples.
3. The word to which the suffix is added must end in a
   single consonant preceded by a single vowel. *Admit, re-
   pel,* and *slap* are examples. *Equip* and *quit* are examples
   too, since the *qu* really stands for the consonant sound
   *kw*, leaving the single vowel *i* before the final consonant.

When the above three conditions are present, the final consonant is doubled and the short vowel sound is retained.

Here are some doubling-of-the-final-consonant words
that are frequently misspelled:

> admit + ed = admi**tt**ed
> begin + er = begi**nn**er
> begin + ing = begi**nn**ing
> brag + ing = bra**gg**ing
> confer + ed = confe**rr**ed
> defer + ed = defe**rr**ed
> equip + ed = equi**pp**ed
> expel + ed = expe**ll**ed
> fad + ism = fa**dd**ism
> fog + y = fo**gg**y
> jog + ing = jo**gg**ing
> lag + ing = la**gg**ing

man + ish = ma**nn**ish
occur + ed = occu**rr**ed
occur + ence = occu**rr**ence
omit + ed = omi**tt**ed
rebel + ing = rebe**ll**ing
red + est = re**dd**est
refer + ed = refe**rr**ed
regret + ed = regre**tt**ed
star + ing = sta**rr**ing
swim + ing = swi**mm**ing
transfer + ed = transfe**rr**ed
(un)forget + able = unforge**tt**able

**Two notes of caution:** (1) If the last syllable of a word is not accented, its final consonant is not doubled when a suffix beginning with a vowel is added. Examples:

aBANdon + ed = abandoned
BANter + ing = bantering

BENefit + ed = benefited
proHIBit + ing = prohibiting

(2) When a suffix is added to a word ending in a silent *e,* the consonant preceding the *e* is *never* doubled. Examples:

come + ing = coming
dine + ing = dining
interfere + ed = interfered

shine + ing = shining
write + ing = writing

These five words are very frequently misspelled because the consonants preceding the silent *e*'s are incorrectly doubled.

# 15B THE DROPPING-OF-THE-SILENT-E RULE

A great many words in English end in a silent *e*. When suffixes are added to these words, sometimes the *e* is dropped and sometimes it is retained. In this section we will consider the rule calling for the dropping of the silent *e*, and in the next, the rules calling for retention of the silent *e*. The basic silent *e* rule is this:

<u>Rule 2</u>   **When adding a suffix beginning with a vowel to a word ending in a silent e, drop the silent e.**

One of the rules in the following section is an important exception to this basic rule, but we must explain the rules separately.

The dropping-of-the-silent *e* rule is also due to the long-vowel, short-vowel principle discussed in the preceding section. Though there are exceptions, most terminal silent *e*'s are doing the job of making the preceding vowel long. That is, if the silent *e* is dropped, the preceding vowel becomes short. Examples:

hate (long *a*)      hat (short *a*)
dine (long *i*)      din (short *i*)

Thus the terminal silent *e* is usually at work. However, because of the long-vowel, short-vowel principle *any* vowel will do the work of the silent *e*, for a vowel-consonant-vowel sequence would still be maintained, making the first vowel long if it is in an accented syllable. Thus when a suffix beginning with a vowel is added to a word ending in a silent *e*, the silent *e* is no longer needed because the vowel of the suffix will do the work of the silent *e*, which therefore can be dropped. Hence we have the basic silent *e* rule.

Here are examples of the rule in action:

dine + ing = dining              shine + ing = shining
write + ing = writing            interfere + ed = interfered
guide + ance = guidance          create + ive = creative
mange + y = mangy                shine + y = shiny
condole + ence = condolence      fame + ous = famous
bite + ing = biting              confuse + ing = confusing

In words like these the long-vowel sound is preserved because a vowel-consonant-vowel sequence is maintained.

Some words in English, however, end in silent *e*'s that do no work, but the rule still applies to them. Examples:

come + ing = coming              imagine + ative = imaginative
hypocrite + ical = hypocritical  pursue + ing = pursuing

The silent *e*'s in these words do not make the preceding vowels long; they are just part of the many irregularities in English spelling. Still, the basic rule applies to them.

# 15C THE RETENTION-OF-THE-SILENT-E RULES

There are two rules for retaining silent *e*'s when suffixes are added. The first is an important exception to the basic rule in the previous section.

<u>Rule 3</u> **When adding the suffix *able, ous,* or *ance* to a word that ends in a silent *e* preceded by a *c* or *g*, retain the silent *e*.**

This rule, too, is based on important phonetic principles in English spelling. Both the *c* and the *g* are used for spelling two entirely different sounds.* First we will consider the *c*, which (with a few exceptions) is pronounced either as an *s*, as in *city*, or as a *k*, as in *cable*. The *c* pronounced as an *s* is called a soft *c*, and the *c* pronounced as a *k* is called a hard *c*. A *c* is almost always soft when it is followed by an *e*, *i*, or *y*, and it is almost always hard when it is followed by an *a*, *o*, or *u* or when it is the last letter of a word or syllable. Thus when a word ends in a silent *e* preceded by a *c*, the silent *e* is doing the job of making the *c* soft. For example, the *c* is soft in *service*, but if the silent *e* is dropped, we would pronounce the remainder *ser-vik*. Similarly, if when adding the suffix *able* to *service* we dropped the silent *e*, the *c* would be followed by an *a*, thus becoming hard, and we would have the pronunciation *ser-vik-able*. Since we want the pronunciation *ser-viss-able*, we retain the silent *e* so that the *c* will remain soft.

For convenience, here is a repetition of this part of the general rule:

**When adding *able* to a word that ends in a silent *e* preceded by a *c*, retain the silent *e* to preserve the soft *c* sound.**

---

* In addition the *c* has a *ch* sound in some imported words, such as *cello* and *concerto*, and is silent in some other words, such as *indict* and *muscle*. *Ch* is a single sound unlike the usual sounds *c* stands for. Also, there are some complex aspects of *g* that we will not explain, for they are not involved in the rule we are discussing.

Here are typical examples:

| | |
|---|---|
| replace + able = replaceable | notice + able = noticeable |
| trace + able = traceable | peace + able = peaceable |
| splice + able = spliceable | embrace + able = embraceable |

Another rule involving the hard *c* is this:

**When adding the suffix *y* or a suffix beginning with *e* or *i* to a word that ends in *c*, add a *k* in order to preserve the hard *c* sound.**

For example, if the suffix *ed* were added to the verb *panic,* the *c* would become soft and produce the pronunciation *pan-iced.* So we add a *k* to preserve the hard *c* sound. Here are examples of the main words involved in this minor rule:

| | |
|---|---|
| panic + ed = panicked | picnic + ing = picnicking |
| panic + y = panicky | politic + ing = politicking |
| picnic + er = picnicker | traffic + ing = trafficking |

Many of our words already have the *k*, such as *kick* and *pick.*

Now we will consider the *g*. The hard *g* is pronounced *guh,* as in *got* and *begin.* The soft *g* is pronounced as a *j*, as in *gin* and *gyp.* The two sounds of *g* do not follow regular phonetic principles to the extent that the two sounds of *c* do, for the *g* is sometimes soft and sometimes hard when followed by *e* or *i*. However, the *g* is virtually always soft when followed by a silent *e* and virtually always hard when followed by *a, o,* or *u* or when it is the final letter of a word. Thus we have this part of the general rule:

**When adding *able, ous,* or *ance* to a word ending in a silent *e* preceded by a *g*, retain the silent *e* to preserve the soft *g* sound.**

For example, *arrange* has a soft *g*. But if when adding *able* to *arrange* we dropped the silent *e,* the pronunciation would be *ar-rang-able.* Thus we keep the silent *e* to preserve the soft *g* sound: *ar-range-able.* Here are other examples:

| | |
|---|---|
| courage + ous = courageous | stage + able = stageable |
| outrage + ous = outrageous | charge + able = chargeable |
| advantage + ous = advantageous | change + able = changeable |

Now the second rule for retention of the silent *e:*

**Rule 4   When adding a suffix beginning with a consonant to a word ending in a silent e, retain the silent e.**

The long-vowel, short-vowel principle makes this rule necessary. For example, the silent *e* in *fate* makes the *a* long. If the silent *e* were dropped when the suffix *ful* is added, the pronunciation would be *fat-ful.* Here are other examples of the rule in action:

| | |
|---|---|
| like + ness = likeness | hate + ful = hateful |
| late + ly = lately | safe + ty = safety |
| complete + ly = completely | care + less = careless |

The *e* must be retained to prevent such pronunciations as *lik-ness* and *lat-ly.*

Sometimes the final silent *e* does not make the preceding vowel long, but the rule still holds. Examples:

immediate + ly = immediately
appropriate + ly = appropriately
approximate + ly = approximately
delicate + ly = delicately

Misspellings due to the dropping of the silent *e* when adding *ly* are quite common.

There are a few exceptions to the above rule. Here are the main ones:

| | |
|---|---|
| whole + ly = wholly | argue + ment = argument |
| true + ly = truly | judge + ment = judgment |
| awe + ful = awful | |

In these words the silent *e* is dropped even though the suffix added begins with a consonant.

# 15D   THE *Y*-TO-*I* RULE

**Rule 5   When adding a suffix to a word ending in y preceded by a consonant, change the y to i. If the y is preceded by a vowel, do not change the y to i.**

When adding the suffix *s* to make the plural of a noun that ends in *y* preceded by a consonant or when adding the suffix *s* to a verb that ends in *y* preceded by a consonant, change the *y* to *i* and add *es*. Examples:

| | |
|---|---|
| ally + s = allies | try + s = tries |
| reply + s = replies | deny + s = denies |
| harpy + s = harpies | defy + s = defies |

The rule also operates with many other suffixes. Examples:

| | |
|---|---|
| comply + ance = compliance | mercy + ful = merciful |
| cry + er = crier | easy + ly = easily |
| dry + est = driest | lonely + ness = loneliness |

The rule does not apply when the suffix is *ing* or *ist.* Examples:

| | |
|---|---|
| study + ing = studying | worry + ing = worrying |
| hurry + ing = hurrying | copy + ist = copyist |

In these words the *y* is *never* dropped; misspellings such as *studing* for *studying* are common.

There are a number of exceptions to the rule, all of them involving one-syllable words. Here are the main exceptions:

| | | |
|---|---|---|
| shyness | slyly | dryness |
| shyly | wryness | dryly |
| slyness | wryly | dryer (the machine) |

A minor rule the reverse of the *y*-to-*i* rule is this:

**When adding *ing* to a verb ending in *ie*, change the *ie* to *y*.**

Examples:

| | |
|---|---|
| die + ing = dying | tie + ing = tying |
| lie + ing = lying | vie + ing = vying |

For convenience, here is a repetition of the second part of the y-to-i rule:

**When adding a suffix to a word ending in *y* preceded by a vowel, do not change the *y* to *i*.**

Examples:

annoy + s = annoys           valley + s = valleys
convey + ed = conveyed       alley + s = alleys
stay + ed = stayed           donkey + s = donkeys
coy + ly = coyly             boy + hood = boyhood

There are a few common exceptions to this part of the rule:

lay + ed = laid          day + ly = daily
pay + ed = paid          gay + ly = gaily
say + ed = said

In these words the *y* is changed to *i* even though the *y* is preceded by a vowel.

The y-to-i rule does not apply in spelling the plural of proper names nor the possessive form of any noun ending in *y*. Examples:

the Bradys          Betty's car
the Kennedys        one ally's advantage
several Sallys      the company's president

# 15E   THE *IE/EI* RULES

The *ie/ei* rules do not cover many words, but they do cover common words that are frequently misspelled.

Rule 6   **Place *i* before *e* when pronounced as *ee* except after c. Place *e* before *i* after c.**

**Most Important:** This rule covers only *ie* or *ei* combinations that are pronounced as the single long *e* sound. That is, the rule does not apply to such words as *science* and *atheist,* in which the *i*'s and *e*'s are pronounced in separate syllables, or to such words as *foreign* and *friend,* in which the combination is not pronounced as a long *e*.

To spell correctly with this rule you must know everything about a word except whether it has an *ie* or *ei* combination. For example, if you don't know that *receipt* has a silent *p,* you can apply the rule correctly and still misspell the word. Here are some common words covered by the rule:

| | |
|---|---|
| believe | receive |
| chief | deceive |
| achieve | deceit |
| priest | conceive |
| thief | conceit |
| brief | receipt |
| relieve | ceiling |
| yield | perceive |
| niece | |
| tier | |
| mien | |

There are a number of exceptions to this rule, but the only ones that give any trouble can be mastered by memorizing this nonsense sentence:

Neither sheik seized weird leisure.

All five of these exceptions have an *ei* combination pronounced as a long *e* but not preceded by a *c.* (In some dialects *neither* is pronounced with a long *i* sound and *leisure* with an *eh* sound.)

Rule 7     **Place e before *i* when pronounced as a long *a.***

Of course there are various ways of spelling the long *a* sound, but if the word has either an *ie* or *ei* combination, then the writer can know that it is *ei* if the pronunciation is a long *a.* Examples:

| | |
|---|---|
| freight | reins |
| weight | vein |
| neighbor | neigh |
| sleigh | reign |
| heinous | deign |

The words *their* and *heir* may also be put in this group, though the vowel sound in them is not exactly a long *a* in many people's dialects.

# Spelling Lists

## 16A DOUBLE-CONSONANT WORDS

The following words are often misspelled because one consonant of a double consonant is omitted. The double consonants are in boldface.

accidental
accommodate
accomplish
accurate
aggressive
annual
apparatus
apparent
applies
appreciate
appropriate
approximate
attitude

beginner
beginning
biggest
committee
communist
controlled
curriculum
different
disappear
disappoint
dissatisfied
disservice
drunkenness

embarrass
equipped
exaggerate
excellent
generally
immediately
immense
intelligence
intelligent
interrupt
irritable
manner
misspelled

narrative
ne**cess**ary
o**ccurr**ed
o**ccurr**ence
o**pp**onent
o**pp**ortunity
o**pp**osite

planned
po**ss**ess
po**ss**e**ss**ion
po**ss**ible
preferred
roo**mm**ate
stu**bb**orn

su**cc**ess
su**mm**ed
su**pp**osed
su**pp**ress
surrounding
swi**mm**ing
u**nn**e**c**e**ss**ary

# 16B   SINGLE-CONSONANT WORDS

The following words are often misspelled because a single consonant is incorrectly doubled. The single consonant is in boldface.

aband**o**ned
a**c**ademic
a**c**ross
a**l**ready
am**o**ng
am**o**unt
ana**l**yze
an**o**ther
a**p**artment
a**p**ology
be**c**oming
bene**f**ited
bi**t**ing
ca**l**endar
ca**r**eer
co**l**umn
co**m**ing
con**f**used
de**f**ine
de**f**initely
de**f**inition
di**n**ing
di**s**appear

di**s**appoint
du**r**ing
e**l**iminate
ful**f**ill
ho**l**iday
im**a**gine
inter**f**ered
la**t**er
ne**c**essary
o**cc**a**s**ion
o**m**itted
o**p**erate
o**p**inion
pa**r**allel
pri**m**itive
pro**f**ession
pro**f**essor
qua**r**rel
re**l**ative
shi**n**ing
to**m**orrow
wri**t**ing

# 16C   *DE* AND *DI* WORDS

The following words are often misspelled because an *e* is substituted for an *i* or an *i* for an *e*. The *de*'s and *di*'s are in boldface.

| | |
|---|---|
| **de**scend | **di**gest |
| **de**scribe | **di**gress |
| **de**scription | **di**lemma |
| **de**spair | **di**lute |
| **de**spise | **di**sastrous |
| **de**spite | **di**sciple |
| **de**stroy | **di**sease |
| **de**struction | **di**vide |
| **de**vice | **di**vine |
| **de**vise | **di**vorce |

# 16D   OMITTED LETTERS

The following words are often misspelled because of the omission of one or more letters. The letters that are often omitted are in boldface.

| | | |
|---|---|---|
| accident**all**y | char**ac**teristics | family |
| accompan**y**ing | (two) communist**s** | fas**c**inate |
| a**c**quire | compet**i**tion | four**th** |
| advertis**e**ment | complet**e**ly | gover**n**ment |
| appropriat**e**ly | (it) consist**s** | her**oe**s |
| approximat**e**ly | criti**c**ism | hop**e**less |
| aspir**i**n | crow**d**ed | hypocrite |
| ath**e**ist | de**a**lt | imagin**e** |
| barg**a**in | definit**e**ly | immediat**e**ly |
| befor**e** | discipl**i**ne | interest |
| bound**a**ry | envir**on**ment | knowled**g**e |
| careless | everything | laboratory |
| carry**i**ng | experience | likely |
| chang**e**able | extrem**e**ly | literature |

144

loneliness
lonely
luxury
magazine
mathematics
meant
medical
medicine
Negroes
ninety
noticeable
nowadays
numerous
particular

(be) prejudiced
primitive
privilege
probably
quantity
realize
remember
rhythm
safety
(two) scientists
shepherd
sincerely
sophomore
stretch

studying
supposed (to)
temperament
temperature
therefore
thorough
undoubtedly
used (to)
useful
valuable
various
where
whether
whose

# 16E ADDED LETTERS

The following words are often misspelled because of the addition of a letter. The incorrect letters that are often added are in parentheses. (Also see Section 16B.)

among (no *u* after *o*)
argument (no *e* after *u*)
athlete (no *e* after *h*)
attack (no *t* after *k*)
awful (no *e* after *w*)
chosen (no *oo*)
disastrous (no *e* after *t*)
drowned (no *d* after *n*)
equipment (no *t* after *p*)
exercise (no *c* after *x*)
existent (no *h* after *x*)
explanation (no *i* after *la*)
final (no *i* after *n*)
forty (no *u* after *o*)
forward (no *e* after *r*)
genius (no *o* after *i*)
grievous (no *i* after *v*)

height (no *h* after *t*)
Henry (no *e* after *n*)
hindrance (no *e* after *d*)
jewelry (no *e* after *l*)
judgment (no *e* after *g*)
laundry (no *e* after *d*)
led (no *a* after *e*)
lose (no *oo*)
mischievous (no *i* after *v*)
ninth (no *e* after *in*)
pamphlet (no *e* after *h*)
personal (no *i* after *n*)
privilege (no *d* after *le*)
procedure (no *ee*)
remembrance (no *e* after *b*)
similar (no *i* after *l*)
truly (no *e* after *u*)

# 16F   *ANT-ANCE* AND *ENT-ENCE* WORDS

| | | |
|---|---|---|
| abund**ant** | resist**ant** | exist**ence** |
| abund**ance** | resist**ance** | experi**ence** |
| acquaint**ance** | serv**ant** | independ**ent** |
| admitt**ance** | warr**ant** | independ**ence** |
| appear**ance** | | ingredi**ent** |
| assist**ant** | abs**ent** | insist**ent** |
| assist**ance** | abs**ence** | insist**ence** |
| attend**ant** | adolesc**ent** | intellig**ent** |
| attend**ance** | adolesc**ence** | intellig**ence** |
| brilli**ant** | appar**ent** | magnific**ent** |
| brilli**ance** | coher**ent** | magnific**ence** |
| const**ant** | coher**ence** | occurr**ence** |
| domin**ant** | compet**ent** | oppon**ent** |
| domin**ance** | compet**ence** | perman**ent** |
| guid**ance** | confid**ent** | perman**ence** |
| hindr**ance** | confid**ence** | persist**ent** |
| ignor**ant** | consist**ent** | persist**ence** |
| ignor**ance** | consist**ence** | pres**ent** |
| import**ant** | conveni**ent** | pres**ence** |
| import**ance** | conveni**ence** | promin**ent** |
| inhabit**ant** | depend**ent** | promin**ence** |
| pleas**ant** | depend**ence** | rever**ent** |
| predomin**ant** | differ**ent** | rever**ence** |
| redund**ant** | differ**ence** | suffici**ent** |
| redund**ance** | excell**ent** | suffici**ence** |
| relev**ant** | excell**ence** | superintend**ent** |
| relev**ance** | exist**ent** | superintend**ence** |

# 16G   HOMOPHONES AND CONFUSED WORDS

**Homophones** are words that are pronounced alike but that have different spellings and meanings, such as *course* and *coarse*. The following list consists of homophones that cause frequent misspellings and also other pairs of words which are so similar that the spelling of one is often confused with the spelling of the other. Information about the words is also included. The abbreviations used have the following meanings: n. = noun; v. = verb; adj. = adjective; adv. = adverb; pro. = pronoun; prep. = preposition; conj. = conjunction; poss. = possessive; contr. = contraction; sing. = singular; and pl. = plural.

**accept:** (v.) to receive
**except:** (prep.) not included

**access:** (n.) a way of approach or entrance
**assess:** (v.) to estimate the value of

**adapt:** (v.) to adjust to a situation
**adopt:** (v.) to take in or take a course of action

**advice:** (n.) counsel, information, or suggestions given
**advise:** (v.) to give advice or counsel

**affect:** (v.) to influence or have an effect on
**effect:** (n.) the result of an action
**effect:** (v.) to accomplish or execute

**aisle:** (n.) a corridor or passageway
**isle:** (n.) an island

**all ready:** (n. + adj.) everyone is prepared
**already:** (adv.) at or before this time; previously

**all together:** (n. + adj.) all in one place
**altogether:** (adv.) completely; wholly

**allude:** (v.) to refer to
**elude:** (v.) to evade or escape

**allusion:** (n.) a reference
**illusion:** (n.) a false impression

**aloud:** (adv.) audibly or loudly
**allowed:** (v.) permitted

**altar:** (n.) an elevated place for religious services
**alter:** (v.) to change

**always:** (adv.) constantly; all the time
**all ways:** (determiner + n.) in every way

**anecdote:** (n.) a little story
**antidote:** (n.) something that counteracts a poison

**angel:** (n.) a heavenly being
**angle:** (n.) figure formed by the divergence of two straight lines from a common point

**arc:** (n.) a part of a circle
**arch:** (n.) a curved part of a building

**ascend:** (v.) to rise or go up
**ascent:** (n.) a movement upward
**assent:** (v.) to agree
**assent:** (n.) an agreement

**assistance:** (n.) help given
**assistants:** (n. pl.) helpers

**band:** (n.) a group
**banned:** (v.) excluded or prohibited

**beside:** (prep.) by the side of
**besides:** (adv. *and* prep.) in addition to

**boar:** (n.) a male hog
**bore:** (n.) someone who tires you

**boarder:** (n.) one who pays for room and meals
**border:** (n.) a boundary

**born:** (v.) given birth to (always in the passive voice)
**borne:** (v.) given birth to (always in the active voice); carried

**brake:** (n.) a mechanism to stop a vehicle
**break:** (v.) to cause to fall into two or more pieces

**breath:** (n.) air inhaled and exhaled
**breathe:** (v.) to take in breaths and let them out

**canvas:** (n.) a kind of coarse cloth
**canvass:** (v.) to search or examine or solicit

**capital:** (n.) a city that is a seat of government
**capitol:** (n.) a building occupied by a legislature

**censor:** (v.) to prohibit publication
**censor:** (n.) one who prohibits publication
**censure:** (v.) to reprimand or disapprove of
**censure:** (n.) disapproval

**choose:** (v.) to select (present tense)
**chose:** (v.) selected (past tense)
**chosen:** (v.) selected (past participle)

**cite:** (v.) to quote; to charge with breaking a law
**site:** (n.) a location

**coarse:** (adj.) rough; unrefined
**course:** (n.) school subject; a way or path

**complement:** (n.) items which complete
**compliment:** (n.) a statement of praise

**conscience:** (n.) what tells you right from wrong
**conscious:** (adj.) awake; alert

**council:** (n.) a group that deliberates
**counsel:** (v.) to give advice
**counsel:** (n.) advice given

**descent:** (n.) a going down
**dissent:** (v.) to disagree
**dissent:** (n.) disagreement

**desert:** (n.) a geographical area
**desert:** (v.) to abandon
**dessert:** (n.) food

**device:** (n.) a contrivance
**devise:** (v.) to prepare a method or contrivance

**do:** (v.) to perform
**due:** (adj.) used with *to* to specify the cause of something; owing

**dual:** (adj.) twofold
**duel:** (n.) a fight between two

**eminent:** (adj.) famous
**imminent:** (adj.) likely to occur soon

**envelop:** (v.) to cover or enclose
**envelope:** (n.) an enclosure used for mailing

**extant:** (adj.) still existing
**extent:** (n.) the degree of something

**formally:** (adj.) in a formal manner
**formerly:** (adv.) at an earlier time

**forth:** (n.) forward; onward; out
**fourth:** (n.) the one after the third

**human:** (adj.) pertaining to people
**humane:** (adj.) pertaining to compassion or kindness

**its:** (poss. pro.) belonging to it
**it's:** (contr.) it is *or* it has

**later:** (adj.) after a specified time
**latter:** (n.) the last one mentioned

**lead:** (v.; pronounced *leed*) to conduct
**lead:** (n.; pronounced *led*) the metal
**led:** (v.) past tense and past participle of the verb *lead*

**loose:** (adj.) not tight
**lose:** (v.) to misplace; to be defeated

**marital:** (adj.) pertaining to marriage
**martial:** (adj.) military

**maybe:** (adv.) perhaps
**may be:** (v.) possibly may occur

**meant:** (v.) past tense and past participle of the verb
    *mean*
**ment:** not a word

**passed:** (v.) past tense and past participle of the verb
    *pass*
**past:** (n.) an earlier time

**patience:** (sing. n.) calm endurance
**patients:** (pl. n.) those under medical care

**peace:** (n.) not war
**piece:** (n.) a part of

**personal:** (adj.) pertaining to oneself
**personnel:** (n.) the employees of a company or organization

**principal:** (n.) head of a school; money owned
**principal:** (adj.) chief; most important
**principle:** (n.) a rule or doctrine

**prophecy:** (n.) a prediction
**prophesy:** (v.) to make a prediction

**quiet:** (adj.) not noisy
**quite:** (adv.) completely or almost completely

**sense:** (n.) ability to think well; meaning
**since:** (prep. *and* conj.) before this time; because

**stationary:** (adj.) in a fixed position
**stationery:** (n.) paper to write on

**than:** (conj.) used to compare things
**then:** (n. or adv.) indicating time

**their:** (poss. pro.) belonging to them
**there:** (adv.) a place; also used as an expletive to begin sentences
**they're:** (contr.) they are

**to:** (prep.) generally indicating direction
**too:** (adv.) excessively; overmuch
**two:** (n.) the number

**trail:** (n.) a rough path
**trial:** (n.) experimental action, or examination before a court

**vice:** (n.) immorality
**vise:** (n.) a device for holding

**weather:** (n.) the state of the atmosphere
**whether:** (conj.) expressing alternatives

**whose:** (poss. pro.) belonging to whom
**who's:** (contr.) who is *or* who has

**your:** (poss. pro.) belonging to you
**you're:** (contr.) you are

# 16H OTHER TROUBLESOME WORDS

The following common words, not included in the preceding sections, are also often misspelled.

| | | | |
|---|---|---|---|
| a lot | doesn't | marriage | ridiculous |
| actually | eighth | minute | sacrifice |
| against | endeavor | nickel | schedule |
| amateur | familiar | optimism | separate |
| amount | favorite | ours | sergeant |
| article | February | paid | source |
| battalion | foreign | peculiar | speech |
| beauty | grammar | perspiration | surprise |
| breathe | guarantee | practical | technique |
| bulletin | height | precede | themselves |
| buried | hers | preparation | theirs |
| category | hundred | prescription | tragedy |
| children | inevitable | prestige | Tuesday |
| comparative | interpretation | proceed | until |
| condemn | involve | psychology | Wednesday |
| counselor | January | pursue | (one) woman |
| courtesy | library | repetition | yours |

**Note:** A proper name ending in y is made plural by the addition of s (the Darbys) and a name ending in s is made plural by the addition of es, with no apostrophe (the Davises).

# Capitalization

Although practices in capitalization do vary, the following specific rules are adhered to by almost all writers. The name commonly used for small letters is **lower case.**

## 17A RULES OF CAPITALIZATION

For convenience, we will not only use our number-letter system of classification but also will number the rules.

### 17A1 The Basics

Rule 1  Capitalize the first word of each sentence, the pronoun *I,* and the interjection *O,* but not other interjections unless one opens a sentence. In using direct quotations, follow the capitalization of the original author exactly.

## 17A2 Titles of Literary Works

<u>Rule 2</u> **In a title or chapter heading, capitalize the first word and all other words except articles, short prepositions, and coordinating conjunctions.**

Examples:

TITLE OF A BOOK: *The Decline and Fall of the Roman Empire*
TITLE OF A SHORT STORY: "The Capital of the World"
TITLE OF A POEM: "The Death of the Hired Man"
CHAPTER HEADING: The Debate Between Skinner and Foster

## 17A3 Specific School Courses

<u>Rule 3</u> **Capitalize the name of a specific school course but not the name of a general subject-matter area, unless it is a proper name.**

Examples:

I am taking History 17A and American Literature Since 1865, but I would rather be taking courses in chemistry and math.

## 17A4 Proper Nouns and Proper Adjectives

<u>Rule 4</u> **Capitalize all proper nouns and adjectives formed from proper nouns, unless the proper adjective — such as *venetian red* — is commonly spelled with a lower-case letter.**

Consult a dictionary if necessary. A proper noun is the name of an individual of some sort, animate or inanimate. Examples:

| | | |
|---|---|---|
| Sweden | John Doe | Oriental |
| Swedish | New Yorker | Arabian |
| English | Hollywoodish | San Franciscan |
| French | Platonism | Newtonian |
| Yosemite | Mount Rushmore | Statue of Liberty |

## 17A5    Religions and Related Topics

<u>Rule 5</u>    **Capitalize references to the Deity or Deities in all recognized religions, the names of religions, religious sects, divine books, and adjectives formed from these.**

Examples:

| | | |
|---|---|---|
| God | Catholic | Jewish |
| our Lord | Protestant | Mormonism |
| Christ | the Bible | Hinduism |
| Allah | Biblical | the New Testament |
| Christian | Baptist | the Upanishads |

## 17A6    Relatives

<u>Rule 6</u>    **Capitalize the titles of relatives when used with the person's name or as a substitute for the name, but not when the term designating the relationship is used with a possessive pronoun, such as *my*.**

Examples:

The caller was Aunt Helen.
The caller was my aunt Helen.
My mother is a nurse.
We see Grandfather Brown playing golf daily.

Usage varies with terms of relationship used as names in direct address.

"Thanks for the help, son (*or* Son)."
"Oh, Father (*or* father), hurry over here."

## 17A7    Officials

<u>Rule 7</u>    **Capitalize the titles of important officials when used with their names. Capitalize a title used in place of a name to designate a particular individual. Do not capitalize a title that designates an office but not a particular individual.**

Examples:

> **V**ice-**P**resident Forbes
> **S**enator Javits
> **C**olonel Wetzler
> **R**everend Puder
> The **C**ongressman will not be in today. (A specific congressman is understood.)
> The **D**ean left instructions for preparing the memo. (A specific dean is understood.)
> A college **p**resident does not have an enviable job. (No specific president is meant.)
> The office of **m**ayor is vacant.

## 17A8   Days, Months, and Holidays

<u>Rule 8</u>   **Capitalize the days of the week, the months of the year, and official holidays. Do not capitalize the names of the seasons.**

Examples:

| | |
|---|---|
| **W**ednesday | **V**eterans **D**ay |
| **F**ebruary | **A**dmission **D**ay |
| **C**hristmas | **w**inter |

## 17A9   Specific Geographic Locations

<u>Rule 9</u>   **Capitalize the names of nations, states, provinces, continents, oceans, lakes, rivers, mountains, cities, streets, parks, and specific geographic regions. Do not capitalize the names of directions.**

Examples:

| | | |
|---|---|---|
| **U**ganda | **L**ake **L**ouise | **J**efferson **P**ark |
| **A**labama | the **R**ed **R**iver | the **W**est **C**oast |
| **A**lberta | **D**eer **M**ountain | the **S**outh |
| **A**sia | **B**altimore | the **N**ear **E**ast |
| the **P**acific **O**cean | **T**enth **S**treet | Walk **e**ast two blocks. |

## 17A10   Buildings

<u>Rule 10</u>   **Capitalize the names of specific buildings.**

Examples:

| | |
|---|---|
| the **H**aberfeld **B**uilding | the **P**alace **T**heater |
| the **P**entagon | the **L**anguage **A**rts **B**uilding |

## 17A11   Private and Governmental Organizations

<u>Rule 11</u>   **Capitalize the names of private and governmental organizations.**

Examples:

| | |
|---|---|
| the **E**lks **C**lub | the **V**eterans **A**dministration |
| the **A**merican **L**egion | the **P**eace **C**orps |
| **R**otary | the **S**tate **D**epartment |

## 17A12   Historical Documents, Events, and Eras

<u>Rule 12</u>   **Capitalize the names of historical documents, events, and eras.**

Examples:

| | |
|---|---|
| the **B**ill of **R**ights | **W**orld **W**ar II |
| the **A**tlantic **C**harter | the **B**attle of **M**idway |
| **P**ublic **L**aw 16 | the **M**iddle **A**ges |
| the **D**iet of **W**orms | the **R**enaissance |

## 17A13   Brand Names

<u>Rule 13</u>   **Capitalize brand names but not the name of the product.**

Examples:

| | |
|---|---|
| a **F**ord car | **D**ial soap |
| **A**rco gasoline | **M**um deodorant |

### 17A14    Outline Headings

<u>Rule 14</u>    **Capitalize the first word of an outline heading.**

Examples:

    I. **U**ses of the dictionary
      A. **T**o determine multiple definitions of a particular word
        1. **M**ethods of ordering definitions
          a. **B**y frequency of use

### 17A15    Celestial Bodies

<u>Rule 15</u>    **Capitalize the names of celestial bodies and of geographic regions of the moon.**

Do not capitalize the words *earth, world, universe, galaxy, moon,* and *sun.* Examples:

| | |
|---|---|
| **A**rcturus (a star) | **V**enus |
| **H**alley's **C**omet | the **C**rab **N**ebula |
| the **S**ea of **R**ains (on the moon) | **P**hobos (a moon of **M**ars) |

**Exception:** When named as a planet among other planets, *earth* is generally capitalized.

In the solar system **E**arth is between **V**enus and **M**ars.

### 17A16    Abbreviations

<u>Rule 16</u>    **Capitalize abbreviations when the whole word or phrase would be capitalized.**

See Section 14C for other aspects of the capitalization of abbreviations and also for punctuation in abbreviations. Examples:

| | |
|---|---|
| the **UN** | the **U.S.** Army |
| the **NAACP** | **b.** 1891 (born) |
| **CORE** | 120 **h.p.** (horsepower) |
| **O**ct. | **g**loss. (glossary) |

# 17B   MANDATORY LOWER-CASE LETTERS

## 17B1   Centuries

<u>Rule 17</u>   Do not capitalize the names of centuries unless a century is being mentioned as a specific historical era.

Examples:

It was my destiny to be born in the twentieth century.
The Age of the Enlightenment is sometimes called simply the Eighteenth Century.

## 17B2   Common Animate and Inanimate Objects

<u>Rule 18</u>   Do not capitalize the names of foods, games, chemical compounds, general geographical formations, animals, plants, or musical instruments unless they designate specific individuals or kinds.

Sometimes, however, a proper noun, which is capitalized, is a part of the name of a species. Examples:

| | | |
|---|---|---|
| rice | escarpment | violoncello |
| spaghetti | trout | Thompson's gazelle |
| golf | robin | a Canary pine |
| bridge | collie | a Baltimore oriole |
| sulfur dioxide | maple | a game of Scrabble |
| schist | rose | our cat, Princess |
| canyon | piano | Lady Baltimore cake |

## 17B3   Occupations

<u>Rule 19</u>   Do not capitalize the names of occupations.

Examples:

engineer
doctor
professor

## 17B4   Diseases

<u>Rule 20</u>   **Do not capitalize the names of diseases.**

Sometimes, however, a proper noun, which is capitalized, is part of the name of the disease. Examples:

**m**umps
**g**astritis
**H**odgkin's **d**isease

# The Apostrophe

The apostrophe is a mark used in spelling, not a mark of punctuation. Marks of punctuation clarify sentence structure, whereas apostrophes clarify word form.

## 18A THE APOSTROPHE IN POSSESSIVE CONSTRUCTIONS

**Use an apostrophe with a noun in a possessive construction.**

There are two ways of expressing possession in English (aside from simply saying *I own something*). The first and most common is with the so-called **possessive construction,** in which the person or thing doing the possessing comes in front of the thing possessed, as in *Estella's good looks* and *the President's power.* The possessive construction calls for an apostrophe *only* if a noun does the possessing, *never* when a personal possessive pronoun, such as *his* or *your,* expresses the possession. The use of the apostrophe for possessive spellings poses two problems: (1) whether or not an apostrophe is needed, and (2) if so, where it should be placed.

The second way of expressing possession in English helps solve both of the writing problems just mentioned. This second way makes use of a *belonging to* or *of* phrase. For example, *good looks belonging to Estella* and *power of the President* have exactly the same meanings as the two possessive constructions in the previous paragraph. Thus any possessive construction will **transform** into a *belonging to* or *of* phrase meaning the same thing as the possessive construction. The *belonging to* or *of* transformation may sound much more awkward than the possessive construction, but it nevertheless will be meaningful English. For example, *Julie's first date* sounds more natural and smooth than *the first date of Julie* or *the first date belonging to Julie,* but the latter are meaningful English. The transformation proves that the former is a possessive construction and thus requires an apostrophe.

When a construction will transform into a *belonging to* or *of* phrase with the same meaning, it is always a possessive construction and requires an apostrophe (that is, when a noun does the possessing). Thus if you have trouble recognizing possessive constructions, with a consequent writing problem in using the apostrophe, learn to test for the transformation. If the construction you are not sure of will transform into a *belonging to* or *of* phrase, you need to use an apostrophe; if a construction will not transform in that manner, it cannot be a possessive construction and thus must not take an apostrophe.

Here are some examples, with the apostrophes required for the possessive constructions omitted.

> Garys hang-up = hang-up belonging to Gary
> the Ferrises bankruptcy = bankruptcy of the Ferrises
> The Ferrises came. = (no transformation possible)

Since the first two constructions transform, they are possessive and require apostrophes in the spelling of *Gary's* and *Ferrises'*. Since the last construction will not transform, it cannot be possessive, and thus *Ferrises* must be spelled without an apostrophe. The test for the transformation is simple, and anyone who masters it should have no trouble knowing when an apostrophe is needed.

The transformation not only shows that an apostrophe is needed but also tells where to place it. (Remember, an apostrophe never belongs directly above an *s,* but either before or after the *s.*) At the end of the *belonging to* or *of* phrase is the **base noun** that will be made possessive and thus will require an apostrophe. Examples, with the base nouns italicized:

> a Christian's faith = faith of a *Christian*
> Lois's GPA = GPA belonging to *Lois*
> the Arabs' oil = oil belonging to the *Arabs*
> the children's misbehavior = misbehavior of the *children*
> The Harrises stayed. = (no transformation possible)

For the four possessive constructions, the base nouns are *Christian, Lois, Arabs,* and *children,* which, in the possessive constructions, must take apostrophes.

In determining where to place the apostrophe in a possessive spelling, you are not interested in whether the base noun is singular or plural, but only whether it does or does not end in *s.* The simple rule is that if the base noun does not end in *s,* in the possessive construction an *'s* is added. But if the base noun does end in *s,* then in the possessive construction an apostrophe after the *s* gives a correct spelling. Examples:

> Bettys new stereo = new stereo belonging to *Betty*

The base noun *Betty* does not end in *s;* therefore the correct possessive spelling is *Betty's new stereo.*

> the Crosses delinquent son = delinquent son of the *Crosses*

The base noun *Crosses* ends in *s;* therefore the correct possessive spelling is *the Crosses' delinquent son.*

In some nouns ending in *s* pronunciation requires the addition of a syllable (es) that is not shown in the written form of the noun. That syllable for pronunciation is shown in brackets below.

Luis[es] importance = the importance of *Luis*
Iris[es] stagefright = the stagefright of *Iris*

The base nouns *Luis* and *Iris* end in *s;* therefore a correct possessive spelling is *Luis'* and *Iris'*.

There is one alternate possessive spelling that we must mention. If the base noun ends in *s* and is singular, its spelling in the possessive construction may not match its pronunciation. For example, the name in the phrase *Thomas' secret deal* is spelled with two syllables but is pronounced in three syllables (Thom-as-es). In such cases the writer has the option of adding an *s* after the apostrophe (Thomas's). Some people prefer the added *s* because it suits the pronunciation better. Either form is correct. Examples:

RIGHT: Mavis' inheritance *or* Mavis's inheritance

This alternate spelling applies only to singular nouns ending in *s*. If the base noun ends in *s* and is plural, the only correct possessive spelling is an apostrophe after the *s*. Example:

RIGHT: the Lewises' squalling brats = squalling brats of the *Lewises*

**Caution:** An *es* is often added to a noun to make it plural, and the plural noun can then be made possessive by the addition of an apostrophe; but an *es* is *never* added to a noun to make it possessive. Example:

WRONG: Jameses date
RIGHT:   James' date *or* James's date

## 18A1   Possessive Proper Nouns

**Use an apostrophe with a proper noun in a possessive construction.**

A proper noun is the name of a unique individual or thing and is capitalized. A proper noun in a possessive construction must be spelled with an apostrophe. If the proper noun to be made possessive does not end in *s*, in the possessive spelling an apostrophe goes before the *s*. Examples:

RIGHT: Sally's motives for running away are unknown.
We were eager to see Mr. Foster's fifth wife.
Mount Whitney's elevation is 14,495 feet.

If the proper noun to be made possessive ends in *s*, adding an apostrophe after the *s* is correct; but if the noun is also singular, another *s* may be added after the apostrophe. Examples:

RIGHT: The Gonzaleses' in-laws are very proud of Ray.
You should have heard Phillis' (*or* Phyllis's) argument with the Dean.
The auditors found Mr. Bass' (*or* Bass's) mistake.

Sometimes a possessive noun ends a sentence with the thing possessed being understood. Such a possessive noun takes an apostrophe. Examples:

RIGHT: Carol's baby is heavier than Jane's.
This stamp collection is worth more than Mr. Foss's (*or* Foss').

*Baby* and *stamp collection* are understood after *Jane's* and *Mr. Foss's*, and thus those names are possessive.

**Caution:** Never use an apostrophe in spelling the plural of a last name when the name is not also possessive. Examples:

WRONG: The Alvarados' are our neighbors.
RIGHT: The Alvarados are our neighbors.
RIGHT: The Gillises won't speak to the Hargises.

One way to test for the correct spelling is to see what pronoun would be substituted for the last name. If *they* or *them* will substitute, the name is not possessive and must not take an apostrophe. If *their* will substitute, the name is possessive and must take an apostrophe after the *s*.

## 18A2 Possessive Common Nouns

**Use an apostrophe with a common noun in a possessive construction.**

A common noun is most easily defined as one that is not capitalized because it is not the name of a unique individual or thing. A common noun in a possessive construction must be spelled with an apostrophe. If the common noun to be made possessive does not end in *s*, in the possessive construction an apostrophe is placed before the *s*. Examples:

RIGHT: The children's toys are being used as real weapons.
A teacher's work doesn't end at 3:00 each day.
It required six sheep's fleece to make that robe.

If the common noun to be made possessive ends in *s*, adding an apostrophe after the *s* is correct; but if the noun is also singular, another *s* may be added after the apostrophe. Examples:

RIGHT: Those roses' odor is somewhat like a crocus's (*or* crocus').
We trapped two lionesses' cubs on our first safari.
A lioness' (*or* lioness's) cubs are playful and unafraid of humans.
My boss' (*or* boss's) temper tantrums keep us all quiet.

## 18A3 Possessive Indefinite Pronouns

**Use an apostrophe with an indefinite pronoun in a possessive construction.**

A group of words called **indefinite pronouns** function as nouns and may be called noun substitutes. The chief ones that can be made possessive are *one, no one, someone, anyone, everyone, somebody, anybody, everybody, nobody, other, another, one another,* and *each other.* Also the *one* and *body* words are often used with *else,* as in *somebody else.* When one of these words is in a possessive construction, it requires an apostrophe and an *s*. Since none of these words ends in *s*, the apostrophe will always come before the *s*. Examples:

RIGHT: Somebody's nose is going to be bloodied if it gets closer to me.

I couldn't think of anyone's phone number.

Everybody else's habits need reforming.

We should all be concerned with each other's welfare.

You can put it into your mind that anytime you hear the *s* on one of the *one* or *body* words (except *one* itself) or on the *else*, the spelling will virtually always be *'s*.

## 18A4    Periods of Time and Sums of Money

**Use an apostrophe to show a possessive construction with a period of time or a sum of money.**

Words that name periods of time are frequently used in possessive construction in English, and they take apostrophes just as any other nouns do. Examples:

RIGHT: One month's vacation is preferable to two months' salary.

Today's crisis is no worse than yesterday's.

February's weather made me think the year's death was occurring.

An hour's value nowadays seems to be $14, at least for plumbers.

Words that name sums of money are also used in the possessive construction in English and require apostrophes just as other nouns do. Examples:

RIGHT: One dollar's worth of steak won't register on the scales.

I prefer a quarter's worth of gin to two dollars' worth of cola.

There wasn't a nickel's difference in our tallies.

Your two cents' worth will get you nowhere.

# 18B THE APOSTROPHE IN CONTRACTIONS

## Use an apostrophe in a contraction.

In contractions, enter an apostrophe where one or more letters have been omitted. Examples:

| | |
|---|---|
| don't | shouldn't |
| doesn't | o'clock |
| we've | I'm |
| you'll | Henry's here. |
| they're | Everybody's gone. |

Do *not* confuse contractions with personal possessive pronouns. The possessive pronouns are already possessive, and so nothing else—not even an apostrophe—is needed to make them possessive. Examples:

| *possessive pronouns* | *pronoun contractions* |
|---|---|
| its (belonging to it) | it's (it is *or* it has) |
| whose (belonging to whom) | who's (who is *or* who has) |
| your (belonging to you) | you're (you are) |
| their (belonging to them) | they're (they are) |

Also, *never* put an apostrophe in one of these possessive pronouns:

| | |
|---|---|
| yours | ours |
| hers | theirs |

These words are already possessive, as *his* and *mine* are, and must not take an apostrophe.

# 18C THE APOSTROPHE IN PLURAL SPELLINGS

## Use apostrophes in certain plural spellings.

Use an *'s* to form the plural of words used as words, of letters of the alphabet, of abbreviations, of numerals, and of symbols. Examples:

RIGHT:  Don't put too many *if*'s in your proposal.
There are four *s*'s and four *i*'s in *Mississippi*.
Professor Smelly's capital C's look like his 9's.
Joey is more concerned with rpm's than with his girl friend.
The 1700's were good years for aristocrats.
You have too many +'s in your equation.

The apostrophes in these plurals make for clarity. When there is no chance of the reader's being momentarily confused, some writers omit apostrophes in some of these special plural spellings.

**Caution:** Never spell the ordinary nonpossessive plural of a noun with an apostrophe. Examples:

WRONG:  Too many cook's spoil the broth.
WRONG:  Many cooks' are unsanitary.
RIGHT:  Too many cooks spoil the broth.
RIGHT:  Many cooks are unsanitary.

# The Hyphen

Like the apostrophe, the hyphen is a mark used in spelling, not a mark of punctuation. It should not be confused with the dash, which is a mark of punctuation twice as long as the hyphen.

## 19A WORD DIVISION AT THE END OF A LINE

<u>Rule 1</u>  **When dividing a word at the end of a line, use a hyphen and divide only between syllables.**

Never divide a one-syllable word, such as *tw-elve* and *len-gth*. Do not divide a word so that a single letter is left at the end of one line or the beginning of another, such as *a-muse* and *shin-y*. When necessary, consult a dictionary for proper syllabication.

# 19B COMPOUND NUMBERS AND FRACTIONS

<u>Rule 2</u> **Hyphenate spelled-out compound numbers (twenty-one through ninety-nine) and spelled-out fractions.**

If a fraction is unambiguously used with the indefinite article *a* or *an,* do not hyphenate it. Examples:

| | |
|---|---|
| thirty-eight wins | two-fifths of my whisky |
| ninety-two losses | one-half of a loaf |
| our fifty-seventh anniversary | a third of the profits |

**Caution:** Do *not* hyphenate noncompound numbers. Examples:

WRONG:  one-hundred, three-thousand
RIGHT:    one hundred, three thousand

Note that *twenty-four* really means twenty plus four but that *one hundred* does not mean one plus a hundred. It simply tells how many hundreds are involved.

# 19C COMPOUND NOUNS

<u>Rule 3</u> **Hyphenate compound nouns when hyphenation contributes to clarity.**

A compound noun is composed of two or more words that function as one noun. A few compound nouns—such as *son-in-law* and *self-control*—are always hyphenated, and some—such as *the White House* and *cooking apples*—never are. When necessary, consult a dictionary. Here are a few of the hyphenated compound nouns that appeared in one issue of a national magazine:

| | |
|---|---|
| job-hunting | shadow-boxing |
| self-interest | kilowatt-hours |
| dry-goods | globe-trotters |
| well-being | by-product |
| Europe-firsters | passers-by |

# 19D  PREFIXES AND SUFFIXES

<u>Rule 4</u>  **Use a hyphen to separate the following prefixes and suffix from their root words:** *self, all, ex* **(meaning former), and** *elect.*

Examples:

> self‐government for Togo
> an all‐American quarterback
> an ex‐mayor of Atlanta
> the governor‐elect of Texas

Use a good dictionary to guide you in the use of such prefixes as *anti, co, non, pro, pseudo, quasi,* and *ultra.*

<u>Rule 5</u>  **Use a hyphen to separate a prefix when its last letter and the first letter of the root word are the same.**

Examples:

> anti‐industrial          de‐emphasize
> re‐echo                 pro‐organization

Some common words, such as *cooperate,* do not now follow that rule. When necessary, consult a dictionary.

<u>Rule 6</u>  **Use a hyphen to separate a prefix when nonhyphenation might be ambiguous.**

Examples:

> a *co‐op* and a *coop*
> to *re‐collect* the equipment and to *recollect* a story
> to *re‐cover* a sofa and to *recover* from an illness
> to *re‐act* a scene and to *react* to a stimulant

<u>Rule 7</u>  **Use a hyphen to separate a prefix when the root word is capitalized.**

Examples:

> non‐Christian          mid‐August
> un‐American           anti‐Kennedy

# 19E COMPOUND ADJECTIVALS

<u>Rule 8</u>  **Hyphenate two or more words that serve as a single adjectival in front of a noun.**

An adjectival is a modifier of a noun, and all kinds of English words can be combined to function as a single adjectival. Failure to hyphenate such adjectivals will often make a reader stumble momentarily or perhaps waste time figuring out word relationships. For example, this phrase appeared in a national advertisement:

> the new embedded in plastic printed wiring circuit

Probably most readers had to pause to think out the word relationships, whereas if the writer had followed the above rule (plus the rule for separating coordinate adjectives) the meaning would have been immediately clear:

> the new embedded-in-plastic, printed-wiring circuit

Rule no. 8 above is especially important for maintaining clarity in writing.

Here are some examples of rule no. 8 taken from one issue of a national magazine:

| | |
|---|---|
| cradle-to-grave needs | law-school faculty |
| two-fisted gesture | civil-rights battle |
| double-parked car | a soft-spoken type |
| all-too-human attributes | cigar-making firm |
| long-term outlay | an eight-year-old girl |
| state-supported schools | high-pressure steam |

Long compound adjectivals should be hyphenated rather than enclosed in quotation marks. Example:

RIGHT: He took an I-won't-budge-an-inch-if-I-die attitude.

**Note:** When the words which form the adjectival follow the noun, they are not normally hyphenated. Examples:

| | |
|---|---|
| the faculty of a law school | a girl eight years old |
| attributes that are all too human | a battle for civil rights |

<u>Rule 9</u>  When a conjunction is entered into a compound adjectival so that two or more adjectivals are intended, leave a space before and after the conjunction but put a hyphen after the word or words that precede the conjunction.

Examples:

all third▪ and fourth▪grade pupils
all first▪, second▪, and third▪ranked candidates

# SECTION FOUR

## DICTION

# 20

# Appropriate Word Choice

Since writing takes many forms and fulfills many purposes, the words a writer chooses should be appropriate to the purpose. A great deal of slang might be appropriate in a friendly letter from one college student to another but quite inappropriate in a letter of application to be read by some unknown personnel officer. In discussing word choice (which is diction) in this chapter, we are limiting ourselves to the kind of writing usually called for in college—themes, essay exams, reports, and term papers.

Words wholly suitable for such kinds of writing may be classified into two groups: (1) **general-purpose words** and (2) **semiformal words.** General-purpose words are suitable for any writing situation and make up the bulk of most kinds of writing. They include virtually all the structure words, such as *no, some, about, such, however,* and so on, and a great many common content words, such as *house, dress, sentence, hungry, good, common,* and so on and on. Semiformal words are not commonly used in the casual conversation of people of moderate education, but they do occur frequently in semiformal or formal writing. Some examples are *disburse* (for *pay out*), *tortuous* (for *winding* or *twisting*), *subsequent* (for *coming after*), *rectitude* (for *moral behavior*), *rectify* (for *make right*), *altruistic* (for *selfless* or *charitable*), and so on. Your college writing need not be limited exclusively to general-purpose and semiformal words, but you should be cautious in departing from these categories. The following sections give advice about appropriate word choice.

# 20A  SLANG

**Avoid using slang expressions unless you feel that they enrich your writing rather than detract from its effectiveness.**

Slang is language that seems to sprout from nowhere for the purpose of providing lively (and usually young) people with irreverent, racy, pungent, and sometimes off-color words and expressions to use instead of words that they consider stale or stuffy or inappropriate for their social situations. A typical example is *stop bugging me* for *stop annoying me.* Volumes could be written about slang, but the following points are sufficient for this chapter: (1) Slang is not bad language *per se;* it can be very good language when appropriately used. (2) The traditional four-letter obscenities and nonstandard words or constructions, such as *ain't got no,* are not slang. (3) A word—for example, *boogie-woogie*—is not slang unless it has a higher level counterpart in the language. (4) The distribution of slang terms both regionally and socially is extremely complex. (5) Some slang terms, such as *hang-up* and *burn artist,* are admirably effective coinages, but others, such as *lousy* and *peachy keen,* are so limp and colorless as to be offensive to anyone who loves language. (6) Most slang terms are new applications of established words, such as *burned out* for *exhausted,* but a few, such as *floozy* and *snafu,* are completely new coinages. (7) Most slang terms are short-lived, for new generations are constantly rejecting some of the language of older people and inventing new slang terms for their own use. (8) Many slang terms, however, rise to the level of standard diction and thus enrich our vocabulary. *Freshman, tidy* (for *neat*), *club, tantrum, mob,* and many other common words were once scorned as mere slang. And (9) a few slang terms, such as *gab* (idle talk) and *broad* (a woman), linger on as slang for centuries.

To repeat, the advice in this section is for you to avoid slang in your college writing unless you consciously think that a pungent slang term will make a sentence more effective than an ordinary, perhaps staid, term with the same meaning. Examples from student writing, with the slang terms in italics:

POOR STYLE: The preacher acted *real cool* when I told him how *I blew the job,* and I began to feel that I could keep from being *popped* If I confessed everything.

EFFECTIVE USE OF SLANG: Within a day after agreeing to the partnership with Marlin, I realized I had a *pencilneck* on my hands and that the background in mechanics he boasted about was sheer *plastic.*

Of course, the ineffectiveness or effectiveness of a slang term can best be judged in the context of a whole paragraph or paper rather than in one sentence. But in general, slang — which appears occasionally in such high-level magazines as *Harper's* and *The Atlantic* — is most effective when it is sparingly used in conjunction with diction of a generally high level.

# 20B COLLOQUIALISMS

**Though you need not avoid colloquial diction in your college writing altogether, you should use it sparingly. Make an effort to choose some semiformal words, especially when you realize that you had first intended to use words on a low colloquial level.**

The word *colloquial* has nothing to do with *local* but comes from a Latin word meaning "conversation." Thus originally, colloquial diction was considered suitable for informal conversation but not for writing. One might say *I have a bone to pick with you* in conversation but would write *I have a disagreement to settle with you.* But nowadays *colloquial* means informal in both speech and writing. All but one of the good collegiate dictionaries use either the label *informal* or *colloquial* to indicate that a word, or one of its definitions, is considered on a level below the semiformal. However, we need to make two points here: (1) Colloquial words are in no way tainted and are not to be avoided unless a writing or speaking situation is important enough to call for a higher level of diction. For example, a bathrobe is eminently suitable clothing to wear in a bedroom but would be out of place at a formal banquet. Similarly, *let's do away with these grandaddy by-laws* might be wholly acceptable in one situation, whereas *let's rescind these outdated by-laws* might be the kind of phrasing most appropriate for another situation. The point is that levels of diction (excluding general-purpose words) do exist, just as different modes of behavior exist in society (compare a stag party for executives with a business meeting to determine company policy). As a writer you want to choose words which will do most to improve the quality of your writing. For college writing that means using colloquial diction judiciously and striving to use a desirable amount of semiformal diction along with the many general-purpose words you must use.

And (2) there is not only one narrowly-bound level of colloquial diction but a very broad level, stretching from almost-slang to almost-semiformal. For example, *to butter up* (to flatter) is barely above the slang level and normally would be inappropriate in semiformal writing; but *to needle* (to goad or provoke) is close enough to the general-purpose category to pass without question in, say, an article in a serious journal. Thus much colloquial diction should be avoided in any writing of importance and much other colloquial diction often has a secure place even in writing as formal as, say, that of a textbook. As students mature educationally, they become more and more able to judge the levels of diction.

Here are some examples of colloquial diction in student writing, with semiformal revisions:

COLLOQUIAL: In algebra I was able to catch on without beating my brains out, and that made me feel a lot better about trying to go on in college.

SEMIFORMAL: I was able to understand algebra with ease, and that encouraged me to continue my college studies.

COLLOQUIAL: When I thought she was giving me the eye, I got carried away and made a fool of myself by trying some shenanigans in the pool with her.

SEMIFORMAL: When I thought she was showing some interest in me, I responded over-enthusiastically and must have appeared foolish when I tried to be intimate with her in the pool.

COLLOQUIAL: The boys thought they could get away with it by claiming over and over that they had told everything, but they couldn't bring it off.

SEMIFORMAL: The boys seemed to assume that they could avoid the appearance of guilt by repeatedly claiming innocence, but they did not succeed in their effort.

The colloquial sentences in these examples are *not* incorrect or even bad writing. However, the person whose writing vocabulary is limited to such a colloquial level will not be able to compose business letters, memos, reports, and so on of the quality demanded in well-paying jobs of importance. So, though colloquial phrasing is respectable, do not let it dominate your writing.

We should make two more points about colloquial diction. First, much colloquial diction in English consists of phrases that have single-word equivalents above the colloquial level. Here are a few examples:

down in the mouth — glum          put up with — tolerate
make a go of it — succeed         catch up with — overtake
give in — acquiesce               get on with it — continue

If you will *think* about your word choice, you will often find that you can improve a sentence by substituting a single-word equivalent for a colloquial phrase.

Second, we frequently use as modifiers of adjectives and adverbs a class of words known as qualifiers. The ones most commonly used in semiformal writing are these:

GOOD STYLE: **very** irritable        **fairly** expensive
            **quite** incomprehensible        **wholly** incorrect
            **rather** staid        **especially** convincing
            **somewhat** embarrassed        **a little** disturbed

Avoid the following colloquial qualifiers:

POOR STYLE: *real* intelligent        *sort of* peculiar
            *sure* pretty        *kind of* sad
            *plenty* excited        *awfully* conceited
            *awful* bad        *pretty* imaginative

Again, these constructions are not out-and-out errors, but they do produce poor style.

# 20C JARGON

### Avoid jargon in your writing.

The word *jargon* has several definitions, but it is most commonly used to mean writing that is so full of pretentious diction and abstract and technical terms that it is almost incomprehensible, even to an educated person. Here is an example of jargon from a textbook on language:

> Discussions on the possibility of a universal base (as distinct from claims about universal constraints on the form of the base component) have mainly been concerned with whether the elements specified in the rules of a universal base—if there is one—are sequential or not.

Perhaps your teacher can give you an understandable revision of this passage. This writer on language doesn't know what that writer on language meant.

In much writing, technical terms cannot be avoided, and certainly words on a semiformal level should not be avoided (see the second paragraph of this chapter). But a writer on any subject can try to make the meaning clear rather than obscure it with jargon. In your writing you should strive to use a college-level vocabulary, but you should avoid pretentious diction, for that contributes to jargon. Happily, not many college freshmen indulge in jargon, though many graduate students do.

# 20D   CLICHÉS

## Avoid clichés in your writing.

A cliché is an expression that, because of long and thoughtless use, is trite, stale, worn out, and lacking in originality. For example, many people who use the phrase "feed at the public trough" don't even know that, when pigpens were common, they contained troughs to hold food for the greedy pigs, and thus many users of the phrase are unaware of its origin. Clichés are very common and have long lives because most people are too lazy or unimaginative to try to form their thoughts in their own language rather than in hackneyed phrases that are used over and over.

Here are a few examples of clichés:

| | |
|---|---|
| ice water in his veins | a tower of strength |
| the acid test | the crack of dawn |
| the irony of fate | life is what you make it |
| take the bull by the horns | drunk as a lord |
| hard as nails | sober as a judge |
| a chip off the old block | a hasty retreat |
| straight from the shoulder | the calm before the storm |
| sneaking suspicion | better late than never |
| a crying shame | the last straw |
| off the beaten track | green with envy |

As you write, *think* about your word choice and choose words more appropriate for your purpose than clichés.

# Exact Word Choice

PRECISENESS OF MEANING

**Choose words that express your meaning precisely rather than approximately.**

The English vocabulary is probably larger than that of any other language, and consequently it has many synonyms (words very similar in meaning) and very many near-synonyms. Good writers try to choose words that say precisely what they mean, whereas careless writers are content with any approximation. Some examples from student writing, with the inexact words italicized:

INEXACT: Tom Paine was *suspicious* of the *foundations* of Christianity.

EXACT: Tom Paine was **skeptical** of the **theological doctrines** of Christianity.

There is some overlapping of meaning between *suspicious* and *skeptical,* but *skeptical* much more precisely expresses

Paine's attitude. Also, *foundations* is a vague and inexact word for the sentence.

INEXACT: As senator, he *achieved* more good laws than any other legislator in this century, but all he got was *slander* from the press.

EXACT: As senator, he **was responsible for the passage** of more good laws than any other legislator in this century, but in turn he was **libeled** by the press.

One does not really achieve a law but sponsors it or supports it or passes it, and so on. Also, though the point is very minor, *slander* implies oral and *libel* means written or pictorial defamation of character. Consulting a good dictionary is a great aid in learning to choose words with the exact meanings you want.

Finally, here is an example that is not easily revised:

INEXACT: Life itself is based on *productivity* and *advancement,* and without this there would be no *status quo.*

What the student meant is not very clear. Perhaps by *productivity* she meant *achievement,* for the former implies material goods and the latter accomplishments of any sort. By *advancement* she perhaps meant *progress,* but either term contradicts *status-quo,* which implies things as they are without change. More careful thought on the part of the student would probably have produced a more exact sentence with, perhaps, important and interesting meaning.

We should say, however, that it is better for you to make mistakes in using the new words you learn than to timidly avoid using a college-level vocabulary for fear of making a mistake. Many students learn a great deal about writing because they *do* make mistakes and then know not to make them again.

# 21B SPECIFIC AND GENERAL WORDS

**Make an effort to use words as specific as your meaning calls for.**

The more specific a word is, the fewer objects or concepts it applies to if it is a noun, the fewer actions or states of being it expresses if it is a verb, and the fewer qualities it signifies if it is an adjective or adverb. Of course a general word is just the opposite. For example, note how specificity increases as you pass from the very general first word to the other words in each of the following lists.

| animal | talk | contented |
|--------|------|-----------|
| quadruped | discuss | happy |
| mammal | disagree | cheerful |
| canine | argue | overjoyed |
| dog | dispute | ecstatic |
| mongrel | quarrel | euphoric |

*Animal* can refer to thousands of species—millions, if insects are included—, but *mongrel* refers to just one type of one species. *Talk* can apply to dozens of types of oral communication, but *quarrel* specifies a narrow range. *Contented* can apply to numerous mental states, but *euphoric* means only the ultimate in emotional happiness. General words are very important in our vocabulary; quite often a writer wants such a general word as *animal* and no other. But the more you can choose specific words, the clearer your meaning and the better your style will be.

Here are some examples from student writing of weak use of general words, with the general words italicized:

GENERAL: Emily Dickinson thought of death as a *good thing*.
SPECIFIC: Emily Dickinson thought of death as a **desirable step into immortality.**

GENERAL: Emily Dickinson is popular because of her *sound* way of *looking at* life.
SPECIFIC: Emily Dickinson is popular because of her **realistic** way of **describing** life.

GENERAL: Now the *course* has been *improved.*
SPECIFIC: Now the **course content better suits the students' needs.**

GENERAL: Letting eighteen-year-olds drink alcohol *causes problems.*
SPECIFIC: Letting eighteen-year-olds drink alcohol **increases traffic accidents and fights among youths.**

Choosing specific diction calls for thought. The tendency of beginning writers is to use the first words that come into their heads, but more experienced writers *think* in order to make their word choice more specific.

We should add, however, that often a writer deliberately chooses a general word with the intent of following it up with specifics. For instance, in the last example above the writer could have used the general word *problems* because he then intended to specify what the problems are. (But he didn't.)

# 21C CONCRETE AND ABSTRACT WORDS

**As much as possible, try to choose concrete words for your writing.**

Technically, a concrete word is one that names an object that can be seen or touched, such as *book* or *kitten.* An abstract word is one that names a concept, such as *socialism* or *devotion,* or a quality apart from the object that can possess it, such as *beauty* or *gracefulness.* All concrete words can form images in the mind; that is, if you hear or read the word *horse* you have no trouble visualizing one in your mind's eye. An abstract word cannot directly form an image in one's mind. For example, the word *communism,* not being the name of a tangible object, cannot form an image directly; whatever images come into your mind when you read the word are due to associations you have made with the word. Thus an abstraction can form images in readers' minds. For example, such words as *leer, smile, pretty, smooth, kind, song,* and so on are abstractions when they are used apart from the person or thing that can wear a smile or be pretty. But they have much of the image-forming effect of such concrete words as *snake, houseboat, lake, owl,* and so on. The advice for you in this section is to choose, as much as possible, concrete words or nonconcrete words that have strong image-forming qualities.

Here are some examples of sentences full of abstractions, with revisions for concrete diction:

ABSTRACT: The modifications that were effected in the subject's orientation to societal mores transformed the approaches and tendencies of her existence.
CONCRETE: The changes brought about in the woman's behavior altered the color and direction of her life.

ABSTRACT: Cooper observed the large majority of all phenomena with conspicuous nonsuccess in apprehending the nature of reality.
CONCRETE: Cooper saw nearly all things as through a glass eye, darkly.

ABSTRACT: Let us render inoperable those invidious machinations that endeavor to legalize the destruction of our movement.
CONCRETE: Let's defeat the legislative bills that would outlaw our political party.

Abstractions, such as the words *modifications, mores, apprehending, invidious,* and so on in the above example sentences, need not be avoided *per se.* Individually they are good words, and we must use abstractions like them. However, when a sentence is little more than an accumulation of abstractions, it is usually not good writing. Concrete and image-forming diction generally improves clarity and style.

# 21D  EUPHEMISMS

### Avoid overuse of euphemisms in your writing.

A euphemism is a mild or roundabout word or expression used instead of a more direct word or expression to make one's language delicate and inoffensive even to a squeamish person. Probably the most frequently-used euphemism is *passed away* for *died.* The areas that demand euphemisms change over the decades. The Victorians, for example, found it convenient to employ euphemisms for bodily functions and parts of the body that might suggest sex. Even later than 1900 a great many genteel people would not use the words *leg* and *arm* because of their sexual suggestibility and talked instead about a person's *limbs.* For one satirist, *toes* became *twigs.* In our time we seem to need euphemisms for the areas of social and economic standing and war. For example, the poor nowadays are usually referred to, at least in public documents, as the *disadvantaged* or *underprivileged;* the very dull student as *educationally handicapped;* the crazy person as *emotionally disturbed;* old people as *senior citizens;* the sacking of a village in war as *pacification;* retreat in war as *planned withdrawal:* lies as *inoperative statements;* and so on.

No doubt many euphemisms do no harm and are actually useful to keep from upsetting sensitive people. But they can also be harmful in that in politics and war they can be deceptive. All writers and readers should at least know what euphemisms are and not be deceived by them. Most of us, no doubt, would rather hear the phrase *nasal discharge* than *snot,* and we can be amused at the phrase *mature entertainment;* but we should be wary of political euphemisms, so that we don't accept *bring order back to the government* for what it says when it really means *establish a dictatorship.*

# 21E　WORDINESS

### Avoid wordiness in your writing.

Good writing should be concise as well as precise — that is, it should not be rambling and wordy. Sometimes a sentence or passage is wordy because the writer rambles around without trying to make economical use of words. An example from student writing:

WORDY: Faulkner put the ditch in "That Evening Sun" so that when it is crossed, as it is several times, the reader can get the understanding that what is on one side of it is completely separated from what is on the other side. What is on one side is the world of the white people and what is on the other side is the world of the black people.

CONCISE: The ditch in Faulkner's "That Evening Sun," crossed several times by some of the characters, is a symbol of the immense gap between the white and black worlds.

Sometimes wordiness is due to the use of an unnecessarily long sentence constituent. Example:

WORDY: The rock group which was brought to play in the pasture of Mr. Hollis were half-stoned by the time they got there.

CONCISE: The rock group brought to play in Mr. Hollis's pasture showed up half-stoned.

The concise sentence uses constituents identical in meaning but shorter and thus more concise than some of the constituents in the wordy sentence. The clause beginning with *which was* is longer than the equally clear phrase *brought to play; Mr. Hollis's pasture* is less wordy than *the pasture of Mr. Hollis;* and *showed up* is much more concise than *by the time they got there.* It takes thought and revision to compose unwordy sentences, for the human mind seems naturally to indulge in wordiness.

Other kinds of wordiness are known as **deadwood** and **redundancy,** in which the elimination of wordiness usually calls not for a recasting of the sentence but simply for the omission of unneeded words. *Redundancy* means saying the same thing twice, such as *audible to the ear. To the ear* adds no meaning and is redundant because the word *audible* means "capable of being heard by the ear" (some sounds can be heard by machines but not by ears; they are not audible). Here are some examples of student sentences with deadwood or redundancy:

WORDY: I liked the biographical information *about Hardy's life* better than his *fictitious* novels.

CONCISE: I liked Hardy's biography better than his novels.

WORDY: The foreign language department has established a *new* innovation *the purpose of which is* to reduce the time we have to study written material *in the textbooks.*

CONCISE: The foreign language department has established an innovation to reduce the time we have to study written material.

WORDY: A metaphor is one kind of figure of speech *that is not literal* because the two *different* parts of the comparison are *completely* dissimilar *to each other.*

CONCISE: A metaphor is one kind of figure of speech because the two parts of the comparison are dissimilar.

The concise revisions in these examples could be written better, but their aim is to show that deadwood — needless words — can often just be omitted, with a consequent improvement in the quality of the writing.

# Correct Word Choice

In Chapter 21 we discussed the value of choosing words for the exact meaning you want, rather than words that only approximately express your meaning. In this chapter we will deal with the choice of wrong words—words which, if taken literally, do not even approximately express your meaning. For example, if you ask someone for change for a dollar and receive nineteen nickels, your request will have been approximately met; but if instead you receive a handful of pebbles, your dollar's change is not even approximately right but wholly incorrect.

# 22A MALAPROPISMS

**Consult a dictionary, if necessary, to prevent use of malapropisms.**

A malapropism, named after a character in an eighteenth-century play who mangled the language in almost every speech, is simply a word wholly incorrect for the meaning intended but usually having some sort of humorous application, such as some similarity in sound. A couple of examples are *a shrewd awakening* for *a rude awakening* and *you lead and we'll precede* for *you lead and we'll proceed (behind you).*

Here are some examples of student malapropisms, with the malapropisms italicized:

MALAPROPISM: The fans were now supporting our team *voraciously.*
RIGHT: The fans were now supporting our team **vociferously.**

MALAPROPISM: Then I pour the *bladder* on the waffle iron and wait for the golden brown waffles.
RIGHT: Then I pour the **batter** on the waffle iron and wait for the golden brown waffles.

MALAPROPISM: Next in the church service we recited the *B attitudes.*
RIGHT: Next in the church service we recited the **Beatitudes.**

MALAPROPISM: Emerson's was a *neo-Plutonic* philosophy.
RIGHT: Emerson's was a **neo-Platonic** philosophy.

MALAPROPISM: I have been absent for the last week because I am going to get married and have been to San Francisco to get my *torso* ready.
RIGHT: I have been absent for the last week because I am going to get married and have been to San Francisco to get my **trousseau** ready.

Such boners are fairly common because young people often misinterpret the sounds they hear and give no thought to the real meanings of the words they misuse. The most common malapropism, perhaps, is *take it for granite* instead of *take it for granted.* But perhaps the funniest of all is the Sunday school child's singing about *the cross-eyed bear* when the hymn "Gladly the Cross I'd Bear" was sung. The dictionary cannot help you avoid such malapropisms as those, but it can keep you from confusing such words as, say, *tortuous* and *torturous.* The value of your dictionary can't be overemphasized.

# 22B CONFUSED WORDS

**Do not confuse a word with one similar to it in sound or meaning or spelling.**

There are a number of pairs or trios of words in English that are so commonly confused that they cannot be labeled malapropisms, which are seldom recurring. Some of these words are listed in Section 16G for spelling purposes. Here is a brief list of the words most often confused, thus producing incorrect rather than inappropriate word choice.

**accept** is a verb meaning "to receive."
**except** is a preposition meaning "not included."

**all ready** is an indefinite pronoun plus adjective meaning "everyone or everything is prepared."
**already** is an adverb meaning "at or before this time."

**all together** is an indefinite pronoun plus adjective meaning "everyone in unison."
**altogether** is an adverb meaning "completely."

**allude** is a verb meaning "to mention indirectly." *Allusion* is the noun.
**refer** is a verb meaning "to mention directly." *Reference* is the noun.

**anyway** is an adverb meaning "in any case."
**any way** is a noun phrase meaning "whatever way possible."

**beside** is a preposition meaning "at the side of."
**besides** is a preposition or adverb meaning "in addition to."

**broadcast** is a verb with the principal parts *broadcast, broadcast, broadcast. Broadcasted* is nonstandard.

**burst** is a verb with the principal parts *burst, burst, burst. Bust* and *busted* are nonstandard for *burst.* (*Busted* is also a slang word for arrested.)

**cite** is a verb meaning "to mention or refer to."
**site** is a noun meaning "a place."

**colloquialism** is a noun meaning "a word or phrase suitable for informal use."
**localism** is a noun meaning "a word or expression used only in one locality or region."

**complement** is a noun (and verb) meaning "something that completes or makes a whole."
**compliment** is a noun (and verb) meaning "praise given."

**conscience** is a noun meaning "a feeling of right and wrong."
**conscious** is an adjective meaning "awake or alert."

**could of, would of** are nonstandard spellings of "could've (have)" and "would've (have)."

**council** is a noun meaning "an official, deliberative group."
**counsel** is a verb (and noun) meaning "to give advice." *Counselor* comes from *counsel.*

**credible** is an adjective meaning "believable."
**creditable** is an adjective meaning "worthy of praise."
**credulous** is an adjective meaning "willing to believe readily or easily imposed upon."

**delusion** is a noun meaning "a false belief."
**illusion** is a noun meaning "a deceptive appearance or false impression."

**disinterested** is an adjective meaning "impartial or having no personal interest."
**uninterested** is an adjective meaning "not interested."

**farther** is an adverb pertaining to physical distance.
**further** is an adverb pertaining to degree of advancement in ideas, concepts, and so on.

**forecast** is a verb with the principal parts *forecast, forecast, forecast. Forecasted* is nonstandard.

**hanged** is the past tense and past participle of the verb *hang* when it means execution.

**hung** is the past tense and past participle of the verb *hang* for all other meanings.

**imply** is a verb meaning "to suggest or hint."

**infer** is a verb meaning "to draw a conclusion or inference about."

**inside of** is colloquial for *within.*

**irregardless** is nonstandard. Use *regardless.*

**kind of, sort of** are colloquial phrases for *rather* or *somewhat.*

**later** is an adverb or adjective meaning "at a time after a specified time."

**latter** is an adjective (and noun) meaning "nearest the end or the last mentioned."

**liable** is an adjective meaning "responsible or legally bound or likely to occur."

**libel** is a verb meaning "to slander in print" and a noun meaning "slanderous articles."

**lie, lay** See Section 8C.

**loose** is an adjective meaning "not tight."

**lose** is a verb meaning "to mislay or be deprived of."

**marital** is an adjective meaning "pertaining to marriage."

**martial** is an adjective meaning "pertaining to military operations."

**maybe** is an adverb meaning "perhaps or possibly."

**may be** is a verb form indicating possibility.

**moral** is an adjective meaning "right or ethical."

**morale** is a noun meaning "a mental attitude or condition."

**nohow** is nonstandard for *anyway.*

**oral** means "spoken." It is preferable in that sense to *verbal,* which refers to both oral and written language.

**passed** is the past tense and past participle of the verb *to pass.*

**past** is a noun meaning "of a former time" and a preposition meaning "passing beside."

**persecute** is a verb meaning "to harass cruelly or annoy persistently."

**prosecute** is a verb meaning "to bring suit against."

**principal** is an adjective meaning "chief or most important" and a noun meaning "head of a school" or "money used as capital."

**principle** is a noun meaning "a rule or doctrine."

**quiet** is an adjective meaning "not noisy."

**quite** is a qualifier meaning "entirely or almost entirely."

**sensual** is an adjective meaning "lewd or carnal."

**sensuous** is an adjective meaning "characterized by sense impressions."

**set, sit** See Section 8C.

**than** is a subordinating conjunction used in a comparison.

**then** is an adverb of time or a conjunctive adverb meaning "therefore."

For words not on this list, consult your dictionary. Form the habit of relying on your dictionary and not just guessing.

# 22C INCORRECT IDIOMS

**Avoid incorrect idioms in your writing.**

Strictly defined, an idiom is a construction "peculiar" to a language, not understandable from the meanings of the individual words in it, and not literally translatable into another language. For example, *ran across* is a common English verb followed by a common preposition and will make such ordinary sentences as *the football player ran across the field* and *the fire truck ran across the water hose.* But consider *I ran across an old friend.* Here neither the verb nor the preposition has its regular meaning, and the whole would probably produce a hilarious construction if translated literally into another language. In this use, *ran across* is an English idiom.

More loosely defined, idiomatic English is any English phrasing that is natural and normal and clearly understandable to a native speaker of English. However, we normally think of English idioms as containing at least one preposition, or a word that looks like a preposition, and that is the way we will consider idioms in this chapter on correct word choice. Thus if (as once happened) a student should write *this contradicts with my opinion,* we would say the idiom was faulty, for native speakers would write *this contradicts my opinion.* English contains countless true idioms.

Faulty idioms are far more common in writing than in conversation, possibly because the writers are striving hard to express their thoughts in writing and make errors *because* they are striving so hard. Here are some faulty idioms from student papers.

FAULTY IDIOM: Poe has been acclaimed by many *of being* a great writer.
RIGHT: Poe has been acclaimed by many **to be** a great writer.

FAULTY IDIOM: Poe is *attributed to being* the originator of the detective story.
RIGHT: Poe is **considered** the originator of the detective story.

FAULTY IDIOM: Military service should not be *likened with* a prison sentence.
RIGHT: Military service should not be **likened to** a prison sentence.

FAULTY IDIOM: Thoreau would have died for the ideals *for which he was so radically supporting.*
RIGHT: Thoreau would have died for the ideals **which he so radically supported.**

Since faulty idioms are usually nonrecurring (except for some in nonstandard English, such as *listen at me* rather than *listen to me*), no rules can be given to keep you from writing them occasionally. The best advice is for you to think calmly and not be in a panic when you write and to proofread your work carefully. Then you are likely to write idiomatic English, for it is truly native to you (unless English is not your native language).

# 22D OMITTED WORDS

**Do not carelessly omit a needed word.**

Examples:

OMITTED WORD: The man bought the car from me was too naive to check it thoroughly.
RIGHT: The man **who** bought the car from me was too naive to check it thoroughly.

OMITTED WORD: Jane was happy about the outcome but my parents bitter about it.
RIGHT: Jane was happy about the outcome but my parents **were** bitter about it.

In the correct sentences the boldface words are needed.

# SECTION FIVE

# EFFECTIVE SENTENCES

# Faulty Sentence Structure

Good writing is a complex mixture of many components, but at its heart is the sentence. The great English statesman and writer Sir Winston Churchill called the English sentence "a noble thing," and it is a truism that anyone who can write really good sentences can write longer passages well too. Sentences, however, are so complex that many things can go wrong with them. But students can learn to write sentences without faulty structure, and thus we have this chapter on the main kinds of errors in sentence structure.

## 23A MIXED SENTENCE STRUCTURE

**Do not inconsistently shift structure in the middle of a sentence.**

Mixed sentence structure usually occurs when a writer begins a sentence with one kind of structure, forgets that structure somewhere along the way, and completes the sentence with a different, incompatible kind of structure. Here is an example from a student paper:

MIXED STRUCTURE: Just loving someone is a one-way affair and has to have someone love you in return.

The shift in structure which produced this mixed sentence comes after the conjunction *and,* which indicates that either a second independent clause or another predicate parallel with *is a one-way affair* is to follow. But the writer lost his way and either did not bother to proofread carefully or else did not have sufficient sentence sense (see Chapter 2) to see that the result was a nonsentence. A unified structure might have been maintained in either of these ways:

RIGHT: Just loving someone is a one-way affair, and for happiness your loved one must love you too.

RIGHT: Just loving someone is a one-way affair and doesn't mean that you are loved in return.

The first revision has two independent clauses and the second two predicates with one subject. Both represent standard sentence structure, though not necessarily excellent writing.

Here are other examples from student writing of mixed sentence structure, with revisions:

MIXED STRUCTURE: A student who is capable of finding a job and succeeding gives him a satisfaction toward his parents.

RIGHT: A student who is capable of finding a job and succeeding in it feels grateful toward his parents.

In the mixed sentence the writer composed the long but satisfactory subject *a student . . . succeeding* but then failed to provide a predicate with a verb that fits the subject. The revision provides a suitable predicate (although, of course, it may not express exactly what the student meant).

MIXED STRUCTURE: All of these facts boil down to that science is playing a major role in our lives.

RIGHT: All of these facts mean that science is playing a major role in our lives.

In the mixed sentence the student writer failed to compose a subject and verb combination that would take the noun clause *that . . . lives* as a direct object. The revision provides a suitable subject and verb.

MIXED STRUCTURE: Those writers that Poe predicted would never make it, we have never even heard their names in our time.

RIGHT: Those writers that Poe predicted would never make it have never been heard of in our time.

In the mixed sentence the student writer composed the long but satisfactory subject *Those . . . it* and then, instead of providing a predicate for the subject, inconsistently continued with a complete independent clause. The revision changes the independent clause into a predicate that fits the subject.

# 23B FAULTY PREDICATION

**In your independent clauses, be sure that your subject and predicate are compatible.**

The grammatical term *predication* means the fitting of a predicate to a subject to make an independent clause (or sentence), such as—

> The horsy set in our town / snubs people with little money.

The slash (/) separates the subject from the predicate.

When a subject and predicate are not compatible, the error known as faulty predication occurs. For example,

> Courageously / is a time of happiness

is obviously a nonsentence because its predication is faulty; the adverb *courageously* cannot serve as the subject of the predicate *is a time of happiness*—or, for that matter, as the subject of any predicate. Equally a nonsentence is this student's creation:

FAULTY PREDICATION: Through God's creation alone / is the only concept of God that man has.

The prepositional phrase *through God's creation alone* will not function as the subject of the predicate that follows. The student may have meant to say something like this:

RIGHT: The only concept of God that man can have / lies in God's creation of the universe.

However, as is often the case in sentences with faulty predication, what the writer meant to say is not entirely clear.

Here are some other examples from student writing of faulty predication, with revisions:

FAULTY PREDICATION: Financial security and social standing / are arguments presented in favor of parent-arranged marriages.

Since financial security and social standing are not arguments, the compound subject does not fit its predicate. The sentence should read something like this:

RIGHT: Many people / argue that parent-arranged marriages provide financial security and social standing.

Another example:

FAULTY PREDICATION: My reaction to being in a large English class / seemed a little strange and different.

The predication is faulty because it was the class and not the student's reaction that seemed strange and different. A better version:

RIGHT: I felt that the large English class / was a little strange and different.

Two other examples:

FAULTY PREDICATION: Another misconception / is when we try to visualize God.
FAULTY PREDICATION: Characterization / is where I think Faulkner succeeded best.

These are examples of the faulty *is when* and *is where* kinds of sentences. Do not use the *is when* construction unless your subject specifies a time, and do not use the *is where* construction unless your subject specifies a place. Otherwise, such sentences have faulty predication. Better versions:

RIGHT: Another misconception / is that human beings can actually visualize God.

RIGHT: Faulkner's characterization / is the best aspect of his fiction.

Now *misconception* and *characterization* are said to be things that they can be, and the predication is sound.

# 23C FAULTY PARALLELISM

**Make sure that the constituents in any series in your sentences are parallel in structure.**

In sentence structure, parallelism means the use of two or more similar constituents in a series, usually with a coordinating connective between the last two constituents. For example:

RIGHT: **Having no money** but **wanting to attend the festival,** I considered selling my typewriter.

The two boldface constituents are parallel in structure because they function identically and are similar in form.

When two or more *dissimilar* constituents are in a series, faulty parallelism results. An example from student writing, with the constituents in faulty parallelism italicized:

FAULTY PARALLELISM: *If a man is brilliant in a specific field* but *he does not have general knowledge,* he may be useless.

Here a dependent clause and an independent clause are joined by *but,* with faulty parallelism the result. The sentence should read like this:

RIGHT: If a man **is brilliant in a specific field** but **does not have general knowledge,** he may be useless.

Now two predicates (with the subject *man*) are in correct parallelism.

Other examples from student work:

FAULTY PARALLELISM: When we entertain *friends, parents,* and *behave ourselves,* we are praised.

RIGHT: When we **entertain friends and parents** and **behave ourselves,** we are praised.

The incorrect sentence has two nouns and one predicate in faulty parallelism. Two proper sets of parallel constituents are in the correct sentence: the boldface predicates and the two nouns *friends* and *parents* in the first predicate.

FAULTY PARALLELISM: Local color was flourishing, *with Harte writing about California* and *Cable wrote about Louisiana.*

RIGHT: Local color was flourishing, with **Harte writing about California** and **Cable writing about Louisiana.**

The incorrect sentence has a prepositional phrase and an independent clause in faulty parallelism. The correct sentence has two objects of the preposition *with* in proper parallel structure.

# 23D   DANGLING MODIFIERS

**Do not let an introductory or terminal constituent dangle with no word or word group to modify.**

Usually when a sentence opens with an introductory constituent that is not the subject, the constituent modifies the subject that follows. Example:

RIGHT: Having no sixth sense, I was forced to guess at the right answers.

The *having no sixth sense* constituent modifies the subject *I,* and the sentence meaning is fully clear. But suppose the sentence were written in this way:

DANGLING MODIFIER: *Having no sixth sense,* the answers had to be guessed at.

Now the sentence seems to say that the answers had no sixth sense. Since the *having no sixth sense* constituent has no word to modify, it dangles, and the sentence structure is faulty.

Here, from student writing, are other examples of dangling modifiers, with the danglers italicized:

DANGLING MODIFIER: *By bringing children up together in schools of equal opportunity,* they will become friendly.

The children (*they*) are not doing the bringing up, and thus the phrase dangles. Revision:

RIGHT: By bringing children up together in schools of equal opportunity, we allow them to become friendly.

Now the sentence has *we* for the introductory phrase to modify.

DANGLING MODIFIER: *Besides being a thing of security for active people,* shut-ins and hospital patients get pleasure from personal-advice columns.

The shut-ins and patients are not a thing of security, and thus the phrase dangles. Revision:

RIGHT: Besides being a thing of security for active people, personal-advice columns give pleasure to shut-ins and hospital patients.

Now the introductory phrase properly modifies *personal-advice columns.*

DANGLING MODIFIER: The church is a good place to go, *when unsettled in mind.*

The sentence seems to say that the church is unsettled in mind, and thus the terminal constituent dangles. Here is a revision:

RIGHT: The church is a good place to go when you are unsettled in mind.

In this revision the dangler has been altered in structure so that it no longer dangles but delivers clear meaning.

# 23E  MISPLACED MODIFIERS

**Always place a modifier in a sentence so that the word or word group it modifies is immediately clear.**

Most sentences in good writing have a number of modifiers, and the good writer must give thought to the placement of modifiers if the meaning is to be immediately clear. For example, consider this sentence from a news report:

MISPLACED MODIFIER: Collins was told that his services would no longer be needed *by the personnel officer.*

When the sentence is considered in isolation, it seems clear that the personnel officer will no longer need Collins's services (though others in the company may). But the whole report made it clear that the personnel officer was firing Collins. Thus the writer misplaced the modifier *by the personnel officer* and no doubt momentarily confused thousands of readers. The italicized phrase should have been placed after *told.*

Here are some other examples of misplaced modifiers, with the modifiers italicized:

MISPLACED MODIFIER: Your interesting letter regarding the honors program *of December 2* reached me today.

*Of December 2* should come directly after *letter,* for the writer was specifying the date of the letter, not of the honors program.

MISPLACED MODIFIER: They can easily destroy this magnificent creation, which represents 3000 years of careful work *with the press of a button.*

The work was not done with the press of a button. For immediate clarity, the italicized phrase should come after *destroy* or at the very beginning of the sentence.

MISPLACED MODIFIER: I feel that I am going to succeed in all my future goals *today.*

For instant clarity, *today* should come directly after *feel* or at the beginning of the sentence.

MISPLACED MODIFIER: Dickinson says that earth's heaven is nature *in her work.*

The sentence makes no sense unless the italicized phrase is placed after *says* or at the beginning of the sentence.

# Pronoun Reference

A pronoun gets its meaning through reference to some other word or word group, which is known as the pronoun's **antecedent.** Since the pronoun does not have meaning of its own, its reference—or antecedent—must be unmistakably clear if the sentence is to deliver clear meaning. Furthermore, even when its meaning is clear, a pronoun must be properly used if the sentence is to be effective and stylistically acceptable. Sentence effectiveness is easily diminished by faulty pronoun reference.

## 24A REFERENCE TO TITLES

**Do not use a pronoun in the opening sentence of a paper to refer to the title or a noun in the title, unless such use is deliberately intended to achieve a desired stylistic effect.**

Though themes, essays, and term papers should have suitable titles, almost always a paper should be opened as though the title were not stated. Here, from a student's work, is an illustration of how *not* to use pronoun reference to a title:

TOPIC: Write an essay about one of your favorite pastimes.

TITLE: Creating Designs on Ceramics

IMPROPER REFERENCE IN OPENING SENTENCE: When you learn the technique of applying design material to *them,* you are ready to work on your artistry.

The *them* in the opening sentence, referring to *ceramics* (or does it refer to *designs?*) in the title, produces a particularly ineffective sentence and theme introduction. Almost always you should avoid referring to your title in your opening sentence.

Sometimes a careless student will even choose a topic from several written on a blackboard or handout sheet, not compose a title at all, and then begin the paper with a reference to the topic, while the teacher does not know which topic has been picked. For example, after being handed a list of seven topics to choose from, one student once opened a titleless paper with this sentence:

IMPROPER REFERENCE IN OPENING SENTENCE: First, I think *it* should be discussed more before *they* make a decision.

The *it* and *they* in the opening sentence ruined the theme at the outset.

# 24B   AMBIGUOUS REFERENCE

**Do not use a pronoun so that it can meaningfully refer to either of two nouns or word groups.**

Ambiguity means having two possible meanings, and pronoun reference is ambiguous when there is more than one clearly possible antecedent for the pronoun. Example from a student paper:

AMBIGUOUS REFERENCE: I happened to walk into Professor Howard's office when he was bawling a student out. *He* appeared unruffled, but I could tell *he* was angry.

Do the *he*'s refer to the professor or the student? Later sentences made the reference clear, but it was at first ambiguous and thus destroyed sentence effectiveness. A revision:

CLEAR REFERENCE: I happened to walk into Professor Howard's office when he was bawling a student out. **The student** appeared unruffled, but I could tell that he was angry.

The two *he*'s in these sentences are unmistakably clear in their reference.

Sometimes ambiguous reference occurs when a pronoun is only understood and not stated. Example from an advertisement, with the understood pronoun in brackets:

AMBIGUOUS REFERENCE: The trunk on a Dart is actually bigger than the one on many full-sized cars. And a family of five fits inside [it] nicely.

The ad writer intended the understood *it* to refer to *Dart* but it seems to refer to *trunk.* The writer should have put *the car* after *inside.* Also note the inconsistency of specifying *one* trunk for *many* full-sized cars.

## 24C  FAULTY BROAD REFERENCE

**Avoid using *this, that, which,* and *it* with vague, indefinite, or ambiguous reference.**

Broad reference means that a pronoun does not refer to an individual noun but to a whole idea expressed in an independent clause or word group. Broad reference is completely acceptable when it is clear, and, indeed, it is very common. Examples:

CLEAR BROAD REFERENCE: I made an A in American Literature, **which** is hard to do when Professor Fleenor is the teacher.

CLEAR BROAD REFERENCE: We must rewrite our Student Body Constitution. **This** is the only way we can avoid the disintegration of our student government.

CLEAR BROAD REFERENCE: I studied without a break until 1:00 A.M., but **it** did me no good on the exam.

The *which, this,* and *it* clearly refer to whole ideas, not individual nouns, and the broad reference is acceptable, or even desirable.

Often, however, broad reference is vague, indefinite, or ambiguous, and then it destroys sentence effectiveness. First, here is an example from a nationally-circulated advertisement:

FAULTY BROAD REFERENCE: Any food you buy that you do not like or use reduces the amount of your savings, *which* after all is the main purpose of our plan.

The *which* seems to refer to the idea of *reducing the amount of your savings,* whereas obviously the writer had in mind *increasing the amount of your savings.* The common remark "You know what I mean" is no excuse for such bad writing.

Here is an example, taken from a magazine, of faulty broad reference of *it:*

FAULTY BROAD REFERENCE: The odds are that such youngsters will drop out of school eight or ten years later with little to show for *it* but the experience of failure.

The *it* seems to refer to the idea of *dropping out of school,* but the writer really meant the pronoun to refer to *attending school.* The faulty reference destroys the effectiveness of the sentence.

The pronoun *this* seems to be most misused in broad reference in student writing. Example:

FAULTY BROAD REFERENCE: Take for example the TV ad wherein they shave off the sand from a piece of sandpaper. How do we know whether *that* is true? Many people, however, never give *this* a second thought.

The *that* is much too vague in its reference, and the *this* is hopelessly indefinite. A revision:

CLEAR MEANING: Take for example the TV ad in which sand is shaved off a piece of sandpaper. How do we know the shaving is not faked? Many people, however, never give a second thought to the truthfulness of TV ads.

Another example:

FAULTY BROAD REFERENCE: I will not try to convince you that all television programs are worthwhile. *This* is a fallacy.

If a reader pauses to think out the meaning, he will understand that the writer means that the idea that all television programs are worthwhile is a fallacy. But the faulty use of *this* destroys the effectiveness of the passage.

Another:

FAULTY BROAD REFERENCE: *Time* magazine says that it has been said that the generation of the 1970's is degenerate. *This* is not true.

What is not true: attributing the statement to *Time* or *Time*'s reporting or the alleged degeneracy of the generation of the 1970's? The ambiguity of the broad-reference *this* defeats the writer's purpose.

One more example:

FAULTY BROAD REFERENCE: When someone mentions voter apathy, most people think of minority groups. *This* is not true.

The *this* is so indefinitely used that the reader must supply a sentence or two of his own to see that the writer means that voter apathy is not limited to minority groups.

So, take great care with your use of the broad-reference *this,* and also of the broad-reference *that, which,* and *it.*

# 24D REMOTE REFERENCE

**Avoid using a pronoun so far removed from its antecedent that the reader has to pause to determine its meaning.**

Example from student writing:

REMOTE REFERENCE: On the first mild day of spring we decided to go sailing. At the lake we found that some vandals had damaged our boathouse and some gear, but we were able to make quick repairs and thus were not disappointed in our first sail on *it* for the year.

The *it* is so far removed from its antecedent, *lake,* that the reader momentarily stumbles and must reread to be sure of the meaning.

And here is an example from a cookbook:

REMOTE REFERENCE: To enhance the flavor of roast chicken, spill a glass of white wine and sprinkle parsley over *it* while roasting.

Aside from the fact that the sentence seems to imply that the wine may be spilled on the floor and that the cook is roasting, the *it* is too far removed from its antecedent, *roast chicken,* for clear reference.

# 24E   IMPLIED ANTECEDENTS

**Do not use a pronoun with an implied antecedent.**

Pronouns may refer to whole ideas but, in good writing at least, they should not refer to adjectives or to antecedents implied and not stated. Example:

IMPLIED ANTECEDENT: Professor Stansbury is humorous and *it* makes her classes popular.

Though the meaning of the sentence is not obscured, *it* refers to the adjective *humorous,* a stylistically undesirable technique in English, and thus the effectiveness of the sentence is diminished. The reader really is forced to mentally supply the noun *humor* for *it* to have an antecedent. A revision:

BETTER STYLE: The humor Professor Stansbury displays in her classes makes them popular.

Another example:

IMPLIED ANTECEDENT: I liked Hawaii partly because *they* were all so friendly.

The absence of *Hawaiians* as an antecedent for *they* creates a poor sentence.

Two more examples:

IMPLIED ANTECEDENT: "The Second Choice" was about a young girl who fell in love and then lost *him*.

IMPLIED ANTECEDENT: In "The Grass So Little Has to Do" Dickinson seems to envy the simplicity of nature and expresses *it* in the last line of the poem.

In the first sentence, *him* is meant to refer to *lover,* who is not mentioned. The *it* in the second sentence has no noun to refer to. Presumably the writer intended it to mean "envy," but the *envy* used in the sentence is a verb. A pronoun cannot refer to a verb. The sentence can be corrected by substituting "that envy" for *it.*

# 24F  *WHAT* AS A PRONOUN

**Do not use *what* as a substitute for the pronouns *who* and *that*.**

Example:

WRONG: The guy *what* sold me that car was a crook.
RIGHT: The guy **who** sold me that car was a crook.

# Faulty Comparisons

Comparisons, which must consist of at least two constituents even if one is understood, occur frequently in our language, and three kinds of errors are common in their use. (See Section 5D for pronoun forms used in comparative constructions.) These errors diminish sentence effectiveness considerably.

## 25A INCOMPLETE COMPARISONS

**Avoid incomplete comparisons that in effect make nonsensical sentences.**

Aside from the conjunctions *than, as,* and *like* and the prepositions *like* and *from* used to form comparisons, two other words—*other* and *else*—frequently help form comparisons. These comparative words should not be omitted so as to make an incomplete or nonsensical sentence.

True, in advertising copy the *than* part of a comparison is often omitted. Example:

INCOMPLETE COMPARISON: El Ropos smoke more smoothly.

The reader might well ask, "More smoothly than what?" Of course the ad writer intends the reader to understand *than other cigars,* and the reader does understand that. Such incomplete comparisons, however, should be avoided in college writing. For example, don't write such a sentence as —

INCOMPLETE COMPARISON: Attending a private college is different

without specifying what it is different from.

A second kind of incomplete comparison is perhaps even less acceptable because it forms a nonsensical (even though understandable) sentence. This is the kind of comparison that says that one thing is longer or kinder or more extensive, and so on than itself. Example from student writing:

INCOMPLETE COMPARISON: Nixon traveled to more foreign countries than any president.

Since Nixon was a president, the sentence literally says that Nixon traveled to more foreign countries than Nixon, which, if we apply rigorous logic, is nonsense. True, the reader understands the meaning intended, but how much more effective the sentence would have been if written in this way:

COMPLETE COMPARISON: Nixon traveled to more foreign countries than any **other** president.

The *other,* a comparison-completing word, makes a great deal of stylistic difference.

Another example:

INCOMPLETE COMPARISON: My father has captured more mountain lions than anybody in our county.

The student's father presumably lives in "our county." Thus the sentence says her father has captured more mountain lions than her father, which is logical nonsense. The comparison-completing word *else* makes the sentence much more effective:

COMPLETE COMPARISON: My father has captured more mountain lions than anybody **else** in our county.

Now the comparison is complete and the sentence much improved.

Remember not to omit the words *other* and *else* in comparisons that call for one or the other of them.

# 25B    FALSE COMPARISONS

**Do not compose sentences that express false comparisons.**

A comparison says that one thing is similar to, greater or lesser than, or different from another. But when the two parts of the comparison are incompatible for comparative purposes, a false comparison occurs and produces a bad sentence. Example:

FALSE COMPARISON: I was searching for a tent like the American Indian.

The sentence is literally comparing a tent with a human being, an absurdity that destroys the effectiveness of the sentence completely. The writer really meant this:

TRUE COMPARISON: I was searching for a tent like the American Indian's.

The American Indian probably had many kinds of tents, but at least now the sentence compares a tent to a tent (*tent* is understood after *American Indian's*) and the false comparison is eliminated.

Here are some other examples:

FALSE COMPARISON: We were searching for a painting more like Van Gogh.

FALSE COMPARISON: My uncle farms like the nineteenth century.
FALSE COMPARISON: Today's students' behavior is just like their parents.

Was Van Gogh a painting? Did the nineteenth century farm? Is behavior a parent? No. The sentences should express true comparisons:

TRUE COMPARISON: We were searching for a painting more like Van Gogh's.
TRUE COMPARISON: My uncle farms as farmers did in the nineteenth century.
TRUE COMPARISON: Today's students' behavior is just like their parents'.

In the first sentence, *paintings* is understood after *Van Gogh's;* in the third, *behavior* is understood after *parents'.* All three of these true comparisons have eliminated the illogicality of the three faulty sentences.

# 25C  OMITTED COMPARATIVE WORDS

**In a double comparison, do not omit a needed comparative word, such as *than* or *as*.**

Sometimes a double comparison calls for two different comparative words, and careless writers often omit one of the two. Example from a student paper:

OMITTED COMPARATIVE WORD: Professor Tilley is as helpful to us students or maybe more helpful than any of the counselors.

One part of the double comparison is intended to say that Professor Tilley is *as helpful as* and the other part *more helpful than.* But the student carelessly omitted the needed second *as.* Revision:

COMPLETE DOUBLE COMPARISON: Professor Tilley is as helpful to us students **as,** or maybe more helpful than, any of the counselors.

The *as* provides the needed completion. Another example:

OMITTED COMPARATIVE WORD: Sara is more beautiful, or at least as
   beautiful as, the Homecoming Queen.

COMPLETE DOUBLE COMPARISON: Sara is more beautiful **than,** or at
   least as beautiful as, the Homecoming Queen.

In the revision the needed comparative word *than* is added
and the effectiveness of the sentence restored.

# 26

# Mature
# and Well-Formed
# Sentences

Avoiding errors and weaknesses in writing is important, but such successful avoidance does not guarantee good writing. Various positive qualities in a writer's sentences are also needed if the writing is to be of good quality. Our point here can be made clearer by drawing a comparison with marriage. In marriage, it is desirable for the partners to avoid quarrels, fights, and other conflicts. But does such avoidance guarantee a happy marriage? No. In addition to avoiding, as much as possible, various conflicts, the partners need to show affection for each other, to love, to share, to be delighted, at least part of the time, with each other's company. The positive and the negative: both are important in many aspects of human behavior. In this chapter we will discuss the sentence from various positive points of view.

# 26A SENTENCE EXPANSIONS

**Strive to achieve maturity of sentence structure; avoid excessive use of short, simple sentences.**

Though short, simple sentences have their place in good writing and are often needed for the writer to achieve a desired effect, most sentences in good writing are composed of more than one simple independent clause. Various kinds of sentence expansions (large sentence constituents) allow us to express two or more full ideas in one well-composed sentence. Little children write mostly in run-on simple sentences, but mature adults do not, for their command of language — including sentence structure — grows as they grow out of childhood. For example, a child might write —

> I found a nickel and I kept it and I went as soon as I could to the store and bought some candy and I didn't want to lose that nickel.

But a person who has matured in his language usage would try to *compose* a sentence with various sentence expansions attached to one or two independent clauses. Example:

> Having decided to keep the nickel I found, I rushed to the store to buy some candy, taking care not to lose the nickel myself.

The foregoing is an extremely simple illustration, but it expresses an important point. Good writers give attention to composing mature sentences with various kinds of sentence expansions, or large constituents. It is *not* necessary for a writer to know the grammatical names of large sentence constituents in order to use them well. No one thinks about grammatical labels while writing, though one may write better because of having thought about (studied) grammar in the process of achieving mature language usage. Nevertheless, we need to label the sentence expansions, or large constituents, that we will briefly discuss.

## 26A1    Compound Structures

One of the simplest methods of achieving mature sentence structure is to use compound structures, which means using two or more similar constituents in a series. Almost any kind of sentence constituent can be compounded. For example, often one subject will serve two predicates, allowing the writer not to repeat the subject. Example:

SIMPLE SENTENCES: The fish inspected the bait. The fish decided not to accept it.

COMPOUND PREDICATE: The fish **inspected the bait** and **decided not to accept it.**

The two boldface predicates are served by one subject, *the fish.* Other sentence parts may be compounded too, as these sentences illustrate:

COMPOUND SUBJECT: **The Queen** and **the Prime Minister** attended the launching.

COMPOUND OBJECT: In a rage Ned kicked first **the sofa** and then **the cat.**

You perhaps miss more opportunities than you realize to tighten your style through use of more compound structures.

## 26A2    Appositives

An appositive is essentially a noun-repeater, though in its totality as a grammatical construction it can exhibit many complex features. It is a noun-repeater in that it defines or explains a noun that it is said to be in apposition to. In spite of the fact that the appositive usually (but not always) is in apposition to an individual noun, it expresses a full idea. Example:

SIMPLE SENTENCES: A black hole is an astronomical body of such mass that not even light can escape from its gravitational pull. It is composed of matter so dense that a thimbleful of it would weigh tens of millions of tons on earth.

APPOSITIVE: A black hole, **an astronomical body of such mass that not even light can escape from its gravitational pull,** is composed of matter so dense that a thimbleful of it would weigh tens of millions of tons on earth.

Chances are that you can improve the quality of your writing considerably by using appositives more frequently.

## 26A3    Adjective Clauses

An adjective clause is introduced by one of the relative pronouns (*who, whom, whose, which,* and *that*), which usually has a noun antecedent in another part of the full sentence. Since it contains a subject and predicate, the adjective clause expresses a full idea, but one that is subordinated to an independent clause or a part of the main sentence. Like all the constituents we are illustrating in Section 26A, the adjective clause allows us to *expand* a simple sentence and thus achieve more mature sentence structure. Example:

SIMPLE SENTENCES: The Dean introduced the main speaker. The main speaker was to address us on choosing marriage partners wisely.

ADJECTIVE CLAUSE: The Dean introduced the main speaker, **who was to address us on choosing marriage partners wisely.**

The superiority of the structure of the second version is plain.

## 26A4    Adjective Phrases

An adjective phrase is composed of an adjective functioning as a headword, with modifiers clustering around it. Although, since it is a phrase, it does not have a subject and predicate, the adjective phrase, as a sentence expansion, expresses a full idea. Example:

SIMPLE SENTENCES: Otto Knutt was extremely unhappy with his recently-purchased used car. He prepared to palm it off on an unsuspecting friend.

ADJECTIVE PHRASE: Otto Knutt, **extremely unhappy with his recently-purchased used car,** prepared to palm it off on an unsuspecting friend.

Such constituents draw meaning (*Otto Knutt was* in this case) from other parts of the sentence and thus express full ideas.

## 26A5    Adverb Clauses

An adverb clause is introduced by one of the subordinating conjunctions—*because, since, unless, if, though,* and many others. These subordinating conjunctions express such relationships as cause-and-result, contrast, condition, time, and so on between the idea in the adverb clause and the independent clause or a part of the main sentence. Example:

SIMPLE SENTENCES: The ballot boxes had been stuffed. The student body had to conduct another election.

ADVERB CLAUSE: **Because the ballot boxes had been stuffed,** the student body had to conduct another election.

The adverb clause not only has a subject and predicate, which perforce means that it contains a full idea, but also a subordinating conjunction (*because*) to express the proper relationship between ideas.

## 26A6    Noun Clauses

Noun clauses usually do not function as sentence expansions but as subjects or direct objects in independent clauses. However, as appositives they can, and often do, function as expansions. Example:

SIMPLE SENTENCES: The Yazidis' basic belief is that the world is at this time controlled by the devil. This belief derives from their observation of the horrendous state of the world.

NOUN CLAUSE: The basic belief of the Yazidis—**that the world is at this time controlled by the devil**—derives from their observation of the horrendous state of the world.

The use of the noun clause as an appositive produces superior sentence structure. In the first of the simple sentences, the noun clause *that the world is at this time controlled by the devil* functions as a predicate noun and is thus not a sentence expansion.

## 26A7    Prepositional Phrases

Often a prepositional phrase with a complex structure functions as a sentence modifier, and as such it expresses a full idea and is a sentence expansion. Example:

SIMPLE SENTENCES: The college president did not have any idea of how he would quell the disturbance. He walked into the midst of the disputants.

PREPOSITIONAL PHRASE: **Without any idea of how he would quell the disturbance,** the college president walked into the midst of the disputants.

Note that the relationship between the ideas in the simple sentences is not expressed, whereas the sentence with the prepositional phrase does express that relationship.

## 26A8    Verbal Phrases

Various kinds of verbal phrases (the technical names of which you don't need to know) serve as sentence expansions. Examples:

SIMPLE SENTENCES: Iva Notion did not agree with either the Republican or the Democratic policies. She joined the American Freedom Party.

VERBAL PHRASE: **Not agreeing with either the Republican or Democratic policies,** Iva Notion joined the American Freedom Party.

Two points are to be noted here. First, the verbal phrase draws meaning from the other part of the sentence and thus expresses a full idea. Second, though it does not have a connective word to express it, the verbal phrase does express the relationship of cause-and-result between the two full ideas—the disagreeing is the cause and the joining is the result.

SIMPLE SENTENCES:  Basil Metabolism wanted to get admitted to the med school of his choice. He devoted enough time to his studies to be elected Phi Beta Kappa at UCLA.

VERBAL PHRASE:  **To get admitted to the med school of his choice,** Basil Metabolism devoted enough time to his studies to be elected Phi Beta Kappa at UCLA.

Note again that even without a connective word (such as *because*), the verb phrase expresses a cause-and-result relationship between the two full ideas.

## 26A9    Absolute Phrases

An absolute phrase is a construction that has a subject with a nonfinite verb form (that is, a verb form that cannot serve as a sentence verb). Naturally such a phrase contains a full idea. Example:

SIMPLE SENTENCES:  The chances of a stock market crash were high. I sold my hundred shares of Snake Oil Laboratories and put the money in a savings account.

ABSOLUTE PHRASE:  **The chances of a stock market crash being high,** I sold my hundred shares of Snake Oil Laboratories and put the money in a savings account.

As in all our illustrations in Section 26A, the *maturity* of the structure of the single sentence, as opposed to the simple sentences, should be clear to you.

## 26A10    Complex Sentences in General

As we said, no writer thinks about grammatical labels as he or she writes, but the good writer does think about composing sentences of mature structure, even though they may frequently be short, simple sentences. All of the sentence expansions we have illustrated can be combined in an infinity of ways to produce an infinity of different, but well-formed, English sentences. An example, chosen within two seconds from an issue of *Harper's* magazine:

COMPLEX SENTENCE: When, like today, something moves me to get on the Fifth Avenue bus, my eyes invariably fall on one woman who seems, at least to me, the quintessential East Side woman, and her Martian differences quicken in me a sense of myself, a pang of self-recognition.

Though this complex sentence cannot really be called a typical sentence from *Harper's,* it is by no means unusual, and any page from that magazine or any other of good quality will contain several or many sentences of as much complexity. Good readers expect such sentences in their good reading material. In addition to two independent clauses, the sentence contains one adverb clause, one adjective clause, two prepositional-phrase sentence modifiers, and one appositive as sentence expansions.

# 26B EFFECTIVE SUBORDINATION

**Avoid weak coordination of independent clauses; achieve effective subordination.**

Sometimes two full ideas in one sentence are of equal importance and deserve equal emphasis, in which case they are usually coordinated. Examples, with the coordinated constituents in boldface:

PROPER COORDINATION: **At the beginning of the year I considered myself a staunch Republican,** but **later events caused me to adopt the label Independent.**

PROPER COORDINATION: **Being disillusioned by the scandals** but still **approving of conservative policies,** I decided to give up the man but not the Party.

In the first sentence two independent clauses are coordinated with the coordinating conjunction *but* joining them. In the second, two verbal phrases are coordinated. In each case the ideas, for effective sentence structure, deserve to be coordinated, or placed in equal rank.

Sometimes, however, one idea should, for effective sentence structure, be subordinated to another, for coordination of them makes the sentence sound childish. Examples:

WEAK COORDINATION: Personnel policies are administered in a haphazard way, and inequities result.

PROPER SUBORDINATION: **Because personnel policies are administered in a haphazard way,** inequities result.

WEAK COORDINATION: The field was not dry, and the game couldn't start.

PROPER SUBORDINATION: **Until the field dried,** the game couldn't start.

The sentences of weak coordination don't sound right because the two full ideas in each are not of coordinate importance. In the sentences of proper subordination, the boldface adverb clauses carry important meaning, but their subordination to the main clauses makes the sentences sound right—that is, makes them more effective.

# 26C   EMPHASIS

**Compose sentences so that the most important ideas in them receive the most emphasis. Cultivate the active voice.**

Emphasis is achieved chiefly by choosing the most effective words to express an idea (see Chapters 20 and 21) and by placing the parts of the sentence so that the most important ideas receive most prominence. Example, from student writing:

UNEMPHATIC: Teenagers often have disagreements with their parents and the main reason is that the parents are afraid that their children will behave as *they* did when young and they therefore unreasonably restrict their children's behavior.

This sentence has an interesting idea but its parts are strung out in such a way that no peak of emphasis emerges. A revision:

EMPHATIC: Since many parents are afraid that their teenage children will behave as *they* did in their teens, they unreasonably restrict their children's behavior, thereby causing disagreements.

Now all three main ideas in the sentence are adequately emphasized, with the independent clause placed to receive most prominence.

Another example:

UNEMPHATIC: We won the game by a point, though with six minutes left we were down twelve points and down sixteen at half time.

The sentence is unemphatic because it winds down and ends with the least important information. A revision:

EMPHATIC: At half time we were down sixteen points and with only six minutes left still down twelve, but we won the game by a point.

Now the parts are placed so that the sentence rises to a proper peak of emphasis.

Though there are numerous reasons for many sentences to be written in the passive voice, the active voice will provide more emphasis if there is no special reason to use the passive voice. Example:

UNEMPHATIC: Our canoe was capsized by our rivals and so the race was won by them.
EMPHATIC: Our rivals capsized our canoe and so won the race.

The passive voice weakens the first sentence, but the active voice in the revision produces proper emphasis.

You can learn to compose sentences for better emphasis by listening to your sentences with your mind's ear. Listen, and *think* about how your sentences sound.

# 26D CLARITY

**Above all, be sure that what you have written will be clear to the reader.**

In many sections of this book we have discussed writing problems that diminish clarity, and we will not discuss those writing problems a second time. However, this is a section of the book your instructor can refer you to when you have not been fully clear in your writing but have not made one of the specific errors explained in other sections of this book. Here is one example of lack of clarity, taken from a nationally-circulated magazine:

LACK OF CLARITY: Every animal has its place and role in nature's grand design, including the predator. Ecological balance is one of nature's laws. Occasional loss of livestock must be weighed against the good *these animals* [italics supplied] do.

Most readers would be at least momentarily confused when they reached *these animals.* At first a reader may think the phrase refers to *livestock,* but that makes no sense. Eventually, it becomes clear that the phrase refers to *the predator,* but the damage of unclear writing has already been done. Besides, *predator* is singular and *these animals* plural, an inconsistency that contributes to the lack of clarity.

# 26E  VARIETY

**For more effectiveness in your writing, vary your sentence structure as you compose your paragraphs.**

A series of sentences similar in structure, particularly if they are all short, produces monotonous writing. Thus you should not continue one kind of sentence pattern through a series of sentences. Sentence patterns can be varied by changing length, by varying the kinds of sentence expansions used (see Section 26A), by beginning some with the subject and others with introductory constituents, and by occasionally using inverted sentence order (that is, by putting the verb before the subject). Here is an example of a passage with little variety of sentence structure. A revision follows.

MONOTONOUS SENTENCE STRUCTURE: My father was most disturbed by my brief period of experimenting with drugs. He thinks all drugs are bad. He doesn't understand why young people want to experiment. He doesn't remember the pleasure of getting high once in a while. He took me to our doctor to discuss the problem. The doctor came to the conclusion that I had no problem now. My father accepted the doctor's conclusion.

VARIETY IN SENTENCE STRUCTURE: Though I gave him concern about various of my activities, my father was most disturbed by my experimenting with drugs, especially since he thinks all drugs are bad. He is old enough now not to understand why young people want to experiment, and he evidently has forgotten the pleasure (which I am sure he experienced) of getting high once in a while. Because of his concern about my brief use of drugs, he went with me to discuss the problem with our family doctor. The doctor, having a much better knowledge of young people than my father, quickly explained that I now had no problem that should worry my father. Upon hearing this, my father breathed a sigh of relief and showed his old trust in me.

The monotony of the original is eliminated by the variety of sentence structure in the revision.

# 26F TRANSITIONS AND COHERENCE

**Use connectives effectively both within and between sentences.**

Essentially, writing consists of strings of ideas, and relationships exist between these ideas. Often there is no word between sentences or parts of a sentence to express a relationship; the relationship is clear simply because of the nature of the writing. Example:

> Growing weary with his team's many mistakes, the coach called off the practice session.

The cause-and-result relationship between the two sentence parts is fully clear even though the sentence has no specific word to express the relationship: the growing weary is the cause and the calling off is the result.

However, our language has many connective words (co-ordinating conjunctions, subordinating conjunctions, and conjunctive adverbs) and transitional phrases (*for example, in addition, on the other hand,* and so on) that are used to make clear the relationships between parts of sentences and between sentences. Good writers are aware of the connectives and use them wisely and liberally in order to make their writing as clear as possible. The great English writer Samuel Taylor Coleridge said, "A good writer may be known by his pertinent use of connectives." And another great English writer, Thomas de Quincy, said, "All fluent and effective composition depends on the connectives." So be aware of connectives and use them effectively. Connectives provide **transition** between ideas, which in turn helps produce **coherence** in writing. Coherence means that all parts of each sentence and all sentences in a passage stick together, making the writing clear, intelligible, and smooth.

Some examples from student writing:

POOR TRANSITION: The world has much good in it. If I were given the ability to make it better, I would take three steps.

CLEAR TRANSITION: The world has much good in it, **but** if I were given the ability to make it better, I would take three steps.

CLEAR TRANSITION: **Though** the world has much good in it, it could be better, **and** if I were given the ability to make it better, I would take three steps.

POOR TRANSITION: Today's world is moving at a tremendous pace. There are many ways to relieve the pressures of everyday living.

CLEAR TRANSITION: **Though** today's world produces tensions **because** it is moving at a tremendous pace, there are many ways to relieve the pressures of everyday living.

POOR TRANSITION: For a change of pace, a person can read the sports page. The rest of the paper should not be ignored.

CLEAR TRANSITION: For a change of pace, a person can read the sports page, **but** one should not ignore the rest of the paper.

CLEAR TRANSITION: **Though** reading the sports page can give a person a change of pace, one should not ignore the rest of the paper.

The boldface connective words in the sentences labeled *clear transition* express the relationships between ideas, relationships that are not expressed in the sentences labeled *poor transition.* Achieving clear transition through proper use of connectives is one way good writers make their writing coherent, which means that the sentences and parts of sentences flow smoothly together.

# 26G   LOGICAL THINKING

**Avoid sweeping generalizations; strive for logical thinking.**

Of course people are entitled to their own opinions (at least as long as they do not let them harm others), and a composition teacher certainly should not grade a paper down because he or she disagrees with the ideas in it. However, human beings by nature often fall into illogical thinking, and thus when you have written an illogical sentence or passage, your teacher should mark the faulty logic.

The most common kind of illogical statement that appears in themes is the **sweeping generalization,** a gross overstatement of the truth of whatever idea is under discussion. Example:

SWEEPING GENERALIZATION: All students everywhere today are again giving serious attention to their studies and avoiding political activism.

That might seem to be an innocent-enough sentence to appear in a theme, but its logic is faulty because the statement is too broad. It includes all students everywhere, and surely there are many students who are not giving serious attention to their studies and surely there are still many students active politically. Such sweeping generalizations need **qualification,** which means that they should be expressed so as not to overstate the case, or include everybody when everybody should not be included. A revision:

QUALIFIED GENERALIZATION: **A great many** students today in **most parts of the country** are again giving serious attention to their studies and avoiding political activism.

Now the qualifying words *a great many* and *most* take the statement out of the sweeping generalization category. Generalizations are *not* out of place in college writing, but you should always be aware of the need to qualify generalizations that might otherwise be so overbroad as to be illogical.

There are many other kinds of illogic which we do not have space to treat in this book. But in general you should try to use sound reasoning in all your writing. For example, here is a typical bit of illogic from a student paper:

ILLOGICAL: The press should not have treated the Republicans so harshly, because the Democrats were up to just as many dirty tricks.

Now even if the second part of the sentence is true, the whole is still illogical because one group's wrongdoing does not justify another group's wrongdoing. If the Democrats were guilty of crimes during the period the student referred to, they too should have been prosecuted and punished for their wrongdoing. The student would have been much more logical had he written his sentence in this way:

LOGICAL: Though the wrongdoings of the Republicans cannot be condoned, there is evidence of Democratic wrongdoing at the same time, and the Democrats certainly should have been castigated for their crimes too. It is not right for the press to turn all its attention to the crimes of just one party.

Human beings are very prone to illogical thinking, but you can make the content of your papers sounder if you give thought to the logic of the statements you make.

# Index

*Boldface numbers refer to rules, lightface to pages.*

## E

## F

## G

## H

# T

Technical terms, abbreviations for, **14C1:** 123
Technical writing, numerals at beginning of sentences in, **14D:** 127–28
Tense, shifts in, **7C:** 70–71
Terminal constituents
  comma in, **10D:** 90–91
  dash in, **11A:** 102
*Than, then,* **22B:** 197
Third person, **7B:** 69–70
Time, abbreviations for, **14C1:** 122
Titles
  abbreviations avoided in, **14C2:** 124
  as headings, **14B2:** 121
  quotation marks in, **13C:** 112–13
*To be,* subjective pronoun forms after, **5B:** 54
Transitions and coherence, in mature sentence structure, **26F:** 235–37
Typewritten papers, manuscript form for, **14A2:** 117–18

# U

Underlining (italics)
  for emphasis, **14B1:** 119–20
  in manuscript form, **14B1:** 119–20
  of phrases used as such, **14B1:** 119

# V

Variety, in mature sentence structure, **26E:** 234–35
Verbal phrases, **1C2:** 26
  in mature sentence structure, **26A8:** 229–30
  pronoun case forms with, **5E:** 57
Verb auxiliaries, **1A5:** 15
Verb forms, **8:** 75–81

finite, **1B2:** 22–23
nonfinite, **1B2:** 22
Verbs, **1A:** 4–7
  complements of, **1B2:** 23–24
  converting irregular into regular form of, **8B:** 79
  defined, **1A2:** 6
  finite, **1B2:** 22–23
  form of, **1A2:** 7; **8:** 75–81
  intransitive, **1A2:** 7
  linking, **1A2:** 7; **1B2:** 24
  mood of, **1A2:** 9
  nonfinite, **1B2:** 23
  past-participle forms of, **8B:** 78–79
  past-tense forms of, **8A:** 78
  principal parts of, **8:** 75–77
  subjunctive form of, **8D:** 81
  tense of, **1A2:** 7–8
  three categories of, **1A2:** 7–8
  transitive, **1A2:** 7
  voice of, **1A2:** 8–9
Voice
  active, **1A2:** 8
  passive, **1A2:** 9
  shifts in, **7D:** 71–72

# W

Weights and measures, abbreviations of, **14C2:** 125
*We-us* construction, pronouns in, **5F:** 57–58
*What,* as pronoun, **24F:** 218
*Who* and *whom,* pronoun case forms after, **5C:** 55
Word choice, **20:** 177–83
  concrete and abstract words in, **21C:** 187–88
  confused words and, **22B:** 194–97
  euphemisms in, **21D:** 188–89
  exact, **21:** 184–91
  incorrect idioms in, **22C:** 197–99
  malapropisms in, **22A:** 192–93

8
9
F 0
G 1
H 2
I 3

# CORRECTION CHART

| | |
|---|---|
| **ab** | improper abbreviation (14C) |
| **agr** | faulty subject-verb agreement (6A-F) |
| **apos** | omitted or misused apostrophe (18A-C) |
| **cap** | capital letter needed (17A) |
| **cl** | lack of clarity (26D) |
| **coh** | lack of coherence (26F) |
| **com** | omitted or misused comma (10A-J) |
| **comp** | incomplete or false comparison (25A-C) |
| **CS** | comma splice or run-together sentence (3A-C) |
| **D** | faulty diction (20A-D; 21A-D; 22A-D) |
| **DM** | dangling modifier (23D) |
| **DN** | double negative (4C) |
| **frag** | sentence fragment (2A-D) |
| **glos** | glossaries (16G; 22B) |
| **hyp** | omitted or misused hyphen (19A-E) |
| **id** | faulty idiom (22C) |
| **ital** | omitted or misused underlining (14B) |
| **K** | awkward construction |
| **lc** | lower-case letter needed (17B) |
| **log** | faulty logic (26G) |
| **man** | incorrect manuscript form (14A) |
| **MM** | misplaced modifier (23E) |
| **mod** | misused modifier (4A-C) |

# CORRECTION CHART

| | |
|---|---|
| **N** | numeral or spelled-out number needed **(14D)** |
| **org** | faulty organization |
| **P** | faulty punctuation **(9-13)** |
| **¶** | undeveloped paragraph |
| **new ¶** | new paragraph needed |
| **no ¶** | improperly divided paragraph |
| **paral** | faulty parallelism **(23C)** |
| **pred** | faulty predication **(23B)** |
| **pro** | incorrect pronoun case form **(5A-H)** |
| **QM** | omitted or misused quotation marks **(13A-E)** |
| **ref** | unclear pronoun reference **(24A-F)** |
| **rep** | unnecessary repetition |
| **shift** | faulty shift **(7A-F)** |
| **simp** | oversimple sentences **(26A)** |
| **SP** | misspelling **(15-16)** |
| **SS** | faulty sentence structure **(23A-E)** |
| **sub** | subordination needed **(26B)** |
| **var** | sentence variety needed **(26E)** |
| **verb** | incorrect verb form **(8A-D)** |
| **W** | wordiness **(21E)** |
| **WW** | wrong word **(22A-C)** |
| **Λ** | omission **(22D)** |
| **?** | questionable usage or ideas |

# GRAMMATICAL TERMS

0-15-505559-3